WORSHIP RESTORED

Worship Restored

DAVID FELLINGHAM

KINGSWAY PUBLICATIONS
EASTBOURNE

ISBN 0 86065 560 1

Front cover design by Vic Mitchell

Printed in Great Britain for
KINGSWAY PUBLICATIONS LTD
Lottbridge Drove, Eastbourne, E. Sussex BN23 6NT by
Richard Clay Ltd, Bungay, Suffolk.
Typeset by CST, Eastbourne, E. Sussex

Contents

Acknowledgements

I would like to thank Terry Virgo, a dear friend and colleague, for his support and encouragement. Also the congregation and musicians of Clarendon Church, Hove, who have helped the principles in this book become a reality in church life.

Preface

Worship has come very much to the forefront in the body of Christ over the last twenty years. A proliferation of new songs, worship albums and books have helped to revive and renew biblical worship. Styles and forms that have become empty and dead are being exposed as the Holy Spirit is bringing a freshness and creative vitality into church life.

This book examines worship from a biblical perspective. It is for church leaders, musicians and anybody who seeks to make worship a priority in their lives. Some chapters have been written with the specialist in mind: 'Leading Worship', 'Developing the Church's Musical Life', and an appendix on orchestration and songwriting. Although these chapters include some technical musical terms for the initiated, there is enough material in them for the non-expert to gain from.

The relationship between church leaders, musicians, worship leaders and congregation is important for developing a church's worship, and it is my hope that mutual understanding will be gained by a knowledge of the principles governing each facet of the church's musical life.

1

A God of Music

'Why let the devil have all the good music?' may be a catchy
title for a so-called gospel rock song, but is it a fair question?
It is thought that Martin Luther was the first to ask it, as he
sought to introduce simple folk music into worship, breaking
away from the very stylized ecclesiastical music of his day. It
was a question that William Booth, the founder of the Salvation Army, certainly asked. With the aggressive and effective evangelism of the Salvation Army in the latter part of the
last century and early part of this one, there arose a martial
musical style, with brass bands, joyful singing, handclapping
and tambourines. This was the music of the people. A popular
pastime was listening to the band on the prom or in the park.
Musical parades were fashionable. Soldiers, smart uniforms
and ladies in bonnets brought life and vigour to Victorian and
Edwardian England. Melodies were borrowed from public
houses, hymns were put to the popular ditties of the day.
'Champagne Charlie is my name' became 'Bless His name He
sets me free'. 'Here's the good old whisky mop it down, mop
it down' became 'Storm the forts of darkness, bring them
down, bring them down'.

In its day the music and worship of the Salvation Army was

communicating at street level. It was no different from the church of today borrowing from the 'charts' to communicate the gospel. Controversy raged then, just as it does now, over the appropriateness of certain types of music in the church. During the 1960s many young people in the evangelical churches began to use guitars and tambourines, even the occasional drum kit. In 1964 The Joystrings, a group of young people from the Salvation Army training college, released a record called 'It's an open secret' which had minor success in the secular charts, much to the dismay of many older Salvationists who had become musically fossilized in brass banding.

A new style of evangelism began to emerge. That social phenomenon of the 50s, rock and roll, had become an established way of life for the teenager of the 60s. The generation gap grew wider as teenagers' dress, values and particularly music moved away from those of their parents. A proliferation of Christian coffee bars, on-the-road evangelists, and gospel groups sought to bridge the gap between the cultural environment of the church and the cultural environment of the street.

The roots of rock gospel music are embedded in this sincere desire to communicate with a generation that was challenging the values, morals, life-style and culture of its parents. When challenged by Christians who did not understand their music, those involved in this new wave of 'gospel pop' would point to Luther and Booth, saying, 'Why let the devil have all the good music?' The controversy still rages today. With some prominent evangelical leaders endorsing the contemporary Christian music scene, and others so hostile that they have written books denouncing it, there needs to be a clear understanding of music in the light of God's word.

Music is an emotive subject. Prejudice rather than rationality often prevails in forming opinions. This is true both inside and outside the church. We are living in days when, culturally, the generation gap is not so marked as it was. Teenagers of the 50s and 60s are now parents of the teenagers of the 80s.

The baby-boomer generation has lived through rock and roll, folk, the Mersey Sound, the underground, as well as various fusions of classical jazz and rock, Tamla, soul, disco, punk and new wave. Today there is generally a much wider acceptance of pop music across the generations, because such music is now an integral part of our culture. Another important cultural change is that the gap between classical music and pop has now lessened. There is much overlap between pop musicians drawing from classical music, and classical musicians drawing from the world of pop. Andrew Lloyd Webber's *Requiem* is an example of the fusion of these two musical styles which have become so integrated that the work has been acclaimed by pop and classical critics alike.

There is now a broad spectrum of musical taste; all styles are acceptable. The world of advertizing has realized this. We are exhorted to buy a particular brand of bread to the accompaniment of the Largo from Dvorak's New World Symphony. With the funky sounds of a disco beat, we can be persuaded that a particular soft drink is the most refreshing. Musically, anything goes.

This broad spectrum of musical taste is also evident in the Christian world. It is now possible to find on the record and cassette shelves of any Christian bookshop anything from the ethereal vocal purity of the King's College choir with its repertoire drawn from the traditional music of Anglicanism, to the grinding, body-shaking, head-banging, heavy metal sounds of the Rez Band. Each could justify their work as Christian music. From sacred oratorio to Salvation Army band; from the gentle folksy sound of the Fisherfolk to the synthesized electronics of Michael Smith; from the contemporary pop of Amy Grant to the traditional singspirational London Emmanuel Choir, whatever your taste, the choice is vast.

Sadly, prejudice based on cultural background, musical taste and religious upbringing causes Christians to hold strong opinions about what type of music is suitable in the church. With such a broad spectrum of music in our cultural environment, and with this reflected in the Christian music scene, and with such a wide variety of music available, it is important to understand certain principles which will help us to overcome prejudice and also release us from condemnation when we feel the music we enjoy is unacceptable to others.

Is there one specific kind of music that is appropriate to worship? And can the truth be conveyed by this type alone? Is there a Christian music that is essentially different from anything in the secular sphere? A significant development on the Christian music scene has been in the realm of worship. With such artists as Graham Kendrick and Dave Bilbrough, and with the many live worship albums from various Bible weeks and conferences, the church is becoming more and more aware of worship music. The worship album phenomenon has appeared with the charismatic movement. Restoration and Renewal have become synonymous with a freshness and vitality in worship that has broken away from stale and irrelevant church traditions.

David and Dale Garratt were pioneers in contemporary worship with their *Scripture in Song* albums. When Jimmy and Carole Owens introduced *Come Together*, a musical for bringing Christians together, there was a strong element of worship in its content. The skill of David and Dale Garratt lay in taking words of Scripture and setting them to very simple, 'middle-of-the-road' type melodies which had a wide acceptance. However, I believe that the rise of 'worship music' is more of a spiritual phenomenon than a musical one.

During the 60s when the Holy Spirit was moving across many denominational churches, one of the first things to be affected was worship. The outflow of the Spirit-filled life is a desire to worship. It was often found that traditional, formal ways of conducting services were too inflexible to allow for freedom of expression in worship. God was giving the church new songs which expressed what he was doing. With this restoring of the importance of praise and worship, there came a new understanding of the many biblical passages which exhort us to praise the Lord with trumpets, harps, lyres, timbrels, strings, organs and cymbals. The pipe-organ was not the only instrument God was interested in!

Praise and worship albums are now a significant part of contemporary Christian music. Christian magazines even run praise and worship charts. With such songbooks as the three volumes of *Songs of Fellowship*, and the various *Scripture in Song* publications, there are many musical resources available in this particular field. This is causing those involved in leading and accompanying praise and worship to be continually assessing what they are doing both in the light of what God is saying to his church and also in the light of the contemporary music scene.

So far, praise and worship music has been easily recognizable by its simplicity and non-controversial musical style. It has been widely accepted mainly because of its effectiveness in drawing congregations into participation. To teach a new song at a Christian celebration is becoming more and more the norm. Overhead projectors, simple music with chord charts, and an abundance of tapes, all add to the accessibility of worship music.

Those involved in leading and playing in worship need to be aware of two very real problems. One is the commercial hype which is building up around worship music, and the other is the tension between musical styles and tastes. David and Dale Garratt's early *Scripture in Song* albums have a simplicity that any congregation, guitarist or pianist can quickly pick up. Their more recent albums, with strong productions and a much more contemporary pop feel, might cause some people to conclude that worship music is getting too complicated. Leading artists in the field of worship music are continually trying to improve quality of musicianship, content and recording skills. But some are asking whether this isn't taking worship originally intended for congregational use, into the realm of the specialists and away from the congregations and humble musicians who seek to accompany them.

We need to remember that worship is for God. God created music and so he knows what type of music is appropriate for worshipping him.

The creator of music

In the beginning God created everything for his own pleasure. He made everything good. He not only created the material universe—substance to see, touch and taste—but he also created sound.

To stand by Niagara Falls and feel, as well as hear, the rush of that tremendous torrent of water is to enjoy not only the sight but also the sounds of God's creation. The wind rustling in the leaves of the trees, the gentle lapping of the water on the beach, the sound of footsteps on the earth are all examples of the aural phenomenon we call sound. Adam and Eve 'heard the sound of the Lord God walking in the garden in the cool of the day' (Gen 3:8).

God not only created sound, but produced from his creative genius the idea of organizing sound into an ordered form, giving it shape, movement and expression. This is basically what music is. It is a sequence of sounds arranged to make a melody, combined with other sounds to create harmony, moving in a definite time pattern called rhythm. The *Oxford Dictionary* defines music as 'the art of combining sounds, with a view to beauty of form and expression of emotion.'

Music was originally God's idea. The first music heard in the universe must have been the song God gave the angels to sing at the creation when 'the morning stars sang together, and all the sons of God shouted for joy' (Job 38:7). What a glorious and euphonious paean of praise must have echoed around the universe as the heavenly host celebrated in joyful singing and shouting about the marvellous handiwork of a powerful and majestic creator.

God not only created music, but he himself is a musician. The Bible refers to God himself singing, thus showing his love and approval of music as part of his creation. In Zephaniah's prophecy there is an exhortation to God's restored people to express their joy in what God has done for them. God is seen to be in their midst as a victorious warrior, exulting over them with joy and rejoicing over them with singing (Zeph 3:14-17).

In Psalm 18 David expresses praise to God for delivering him from the hand of Saul. This psalm is prophetic, pointing to the coming of the Lord Jesus, his victory over his enemies, and the triumph of the kingdom of God among all the nations. Paul quotes from this psalm in Romans 15:9 and shows that Jesus gives praise to his Father for the gospel coming to the gentiles—and it is praise rendered in song. Another reference to Jesus singing can be found in Hebrews 2:12, in the context of his death for our salvation. Jesus stands in the midst of the redeemed brethren (or church) and sings praise to his Father for the children who have been given to him.

The Bible is full of references to music and singing, and there are many passages which, in their original form, would have been sung. After Israel had been delivered from Egypt and had miraculously come through the Red Sea, Moses and the sons of Israel sang a song of deliverance and victory accompanied by Miriam and all the women, dancing and rejoicing with their timbrels. In Revelation 15 the victorious company of God's redeemed people, each individual with his harp, joins in the song of Moses and of the Lamb. Just as Moses and the children of Israel had a song of deliverance to sing after the Red Sea, so the church has a song of deliverance, rejoicing in the Lamb, who has set his people free from the slavery of sin.

The theme of salvation and deliverance which runs through the whole Bible is accompanied by the music of delivered saints who have a new song of praise put on their lips by God himself. The Psalms give many injunctions to praise the Lord with instruments. God is a musical God. He created music for his own enjoyment as well as ours. He gave all the angelic host musical ability, but before the dawning of the ages one particular angel was given a special ministry in music. His name was Lucifer. The King of Tyre in Ezekial 28 is generally understood as a type of Satan. He is described as a beautiful and splendid heavenly being, 'having the seal of perfection, full of wisdom and perfect in beauty. The workmanship of tambourines and flutes was in him from the day of his creation' (Ezek 28:13, New American Standard Bible, marginal reference). As the 'covering cherub' in the mountain of God, he would have had a leading role in the heavenly worship. Satan, therefore, has a particular interest in corrupting music.

When God created man in his own image he imparted creativity to him, including the faculty of music making. That creativity is now affected by his fallen nature, so the music he creates is tainted with sin. Satan, fallen musician that he is, will do all he can to inspire man to make music for evil and corrupt purposes. Satan is not a creator but a destroyer. He cannot create music of himself, but he can seek to pervert and destroy God's creativity in man. Music in itself is neither good nor bad—it is amoral, but man's use of it gives it potential for either good or evil.

The culture and philosophy of the ancient Greeks has had an important influence on the way we think today. This is true not only in the field of education and politics but also in the realm of music. The Greeks held a view about music which has been called 'the doctrine of ethos'. This view stated that because music was a 'system of sound and rhithm ruled by the same mathematical laws that operate in the whole of the visible and invisible creation', it had a moral quality to it. It was Aristotle who said:

> Music directly imitates the passions or states of the soul—gentleness, anger, courage, temperance, and their opposites and other qualities; hence when one listens to music that imitates a certain passion, he becomes imbued with the same passion; and if over a long time he habitually listens to the kind of music that arouses ignoble passions, his whole character will be shaped to an ignoble form.[1]

The Greek system of music was based on certain scales called modes which the Greeks believed were capable of affecting character and behaviour. Aristotle said that 'the musical modes differ essentially from one another and those who hear them are differently affected by each. Some of them make men sad and grave, others enfeeble the mind; another again produces a moderate and settled temper'.[2]

This moral aspect of music infiltrated into the thinking of the early church:

> The belief that music affected man in different but very definite ways, explains why the study of it was such an essential part of Greek education, for each melody, rhythm, and instrument was thought to exert its own special influence on man's character, a belief which the early church fathers subscribed to.[3]

Although a major influence on the early church was the music of the Jewish temple, with the spread of the gospel into the gentile world there came a cultural influence on the Christians that created a tension which they found difficult to resolve. On the one hand they were teaching their converts to break with everything pagan and sought to wean them away from music which was associated with their pagan past, on the other hand there was a very definite musical influence on the early church from non-Christian sources.

It would appear that the doctrine of ethos had a significant part to play in forming the musical style of the early church as they sought for a purity of expression. There seemed to be a fear that secular music styles would draw people away from Christianity, and a fear of music for music's sake. By the fourth century there was a real conflict between sacred and secular, the dilemma of music in the church—a problem which is still with us today. It may be summed up in the well-known words of Augustine:

> Yet when I recall the tears I shed at the hymns of the Church, in the first days of my recovered faith, and now, too, when I am moved, not by the singing but by the words which are sung (when they are sung in a clear voice and a truly appropriate tune) I admit again the great usefulness of this institution. Thus I waver between the peril of pleasure, and a wholesomeness of which I approve. I am the more inclined, though my opinion may not be final, to approve the custom of hymns in the service, that by the delight of the ears, less sturdy minds may rise to a feeling of devotion. Yet when it happens that the music of the voice moves

me more than the words it sings, I confess myself to have sinned in a way that merits punishment, and then I would rather not hear the singer. Just see my position! Weep with me. Weep for me, those of you who entertain any good within you which can produce action. If you are not one of these, such considerations do not stir you. But you, O Lord my God, hear, regard me, look and pity. Heal me, in whose eyes I am now become a problem to myself. That is my infirmity.[4]

If we understand that music is a facet of God's own creativity and has been given to mankind as a gift, one of those 'all things to enjoy' (2 Tim 6:17) then we may legitimately derive great pleasure from listening to music or making it, just for its own sake. God loves making music, and also enjoys listening to it so much that he has instructed us to sing and make melody in our hearts to the accompaniment of a whole range of instruments. The crucial question is surely not, 'What style of music should we use in worship' but, 'In what spirit are we worshipping?' If we as Christians are freed from sin then we can surely enjoy making music, whatever the style, for God created it.

In posing the question, 'What style of music is suitable for worship?' we must beware of value judgements based on cultural background, taste and religious upbringing. We must beware of applying humanistic Greek philosophy which sees music as an independent moral agent. And we must also beware that we do not see Satan as a being who has creative powers, as he has none of God's attributes and can only seek to pervert God's creativity.

This question must be answered in the light of biblical revelation concerning worship. In the Old Testament the musical priesthood led the congregation with creativity and vitality in both Tabernacle and Temple worship. It is therefore evident that musical creativity had divine approval. Surely the God of the Old Testament, who himself has created music and imparted creativity to his creation, would not have withdrawn his approval of such in the New Testament. There is a wide variety of instruments, rhythms and harmonies that we can employ to bless God.

The New Testament does not give such an explicit description of worship. However, there is clear evidence to suggest that the early church was strongly influenced by worship in the Old Testament. In the next chapter we will explore that evidence and see that although spontaneity and creativity were lost in the later history of the church, there have been times of recovery during outpourings of the Holy Spirit.

2

The History of Worship
in the Church

A commotion in a public place will always attract attention. The Day of Pentecost, forty-nine days after the resurrection of Jesus, was to be a day of considerable disturbance in the city of Jerusalem. The gentle warmth of early summer made this a congenial time for festivities and celebrations. The citizens of Jerusalem had come together for the celebration of the Feast of Pentecost by Jews and proselytes from every part of the Roman Empire, each with their dialect and language.

Suddenly, at nine o'clock in the morning, 120 excited, noisy people disrupted the preparations for the day's festivities. Shock, incredulity, amazement and scepticism would have been the mixed reactions of the crowds as they heard the mighty works of God being declared in a wide range of languages and dialects.

Jesus had spoken of worship in spirit and in truth. The outpouring of the Holy Spirit on the early church produced the initial fruit of praise and worship. The powerful energy of the Holy Spirit transformed those disciples from a timid company behind locked doors into a bold and fearless band. Jesus had ascended and returned to his Father, but now the Spirit had come. The church was born in the midst of a transformed people filled with the Spirit, overflowing in praises as they magnified the Lord.

The curiosity and questions of the people were soon answered as Peter addressed the crowd, explaining what was going on before them. 3,000 responded to the gospel that day. A new era had begun. The believers were quickly established as a community which bore testimony to the risen Lord Jesus.

The infant church devoted themselves to the Apostles' teaching, to fellowship, breaking of bread, and prayer. A sense of awe prevailed as God's presence was experienced through signs and wonders. A strong community spirit engendered a desire to give their possessions for the common good. Each day people were saved and added to the company of believers, and with gladness and sincerity of heart the newly established church gave praise to God.

With thousands of believers in Jerusalem, an area of the Temple known as Solomon's Portico became a gathering place where the Apostles could preach and teach. Large gatherings in the Temple, and small gatherings in homes for fellowship and breaking of bread, meant that the early church grew not only numerically but also in quality of life.

During these formative years the influence of the synagogue could be felt in the assembling of the people together. After the Babylonian captivity the synagogues supplemented the worship at the Temple. There was a synagogue in every town and village in Israel, as well as in every place throughout the Roman Empire where there were Jewish communities.

Worship in the synagogue consisted of the reading from the Scriptures with an explanation and exposition by the rabbi. There were also prayers and the singing of psalms. It is possible that the Levites, who were appointed to serve in the Temple twice a year for one week, brought the influence of Temple worship back with them into the local synagogue. Although history is not clear as to the type and quantity of music in the synagogue services, it seems that during the period after the exile, singing of psalms became an integral part of Jewish folk culture as a means of self-expression. It is reasonable to assume that worshipping God by singing psalms would have become part of synagogue life, especially as the singing of psalms also took place in the home. On the night of the Passover, Jewish families used to sing the Hallel Psalms together. The night before Jesus died, he sang a hymn with the disciples. This was probably the Great Hallel, consisting of Psalms 113-118. They were carrying on the tradition taught to them in their families.

It is against this background that the early church gathered together for their meetings. Large gatherings in the Temple and small gatherings in the home were supplemented with gatherings in the synagogue (Acts 5:42; 13:5, 14; 17:2, 10), especially as the missionary thrust of the church increased. It was Paul's custom first of all to preach in the synagogues, though there was often the opposition of the unreceptive traditionalists to contend with.

Within a short while, the early Christians had to organize themselves into assemblies independent of the synagogues to give full expression to their new-found faith. Much of the synagogue pattern remained, with prayer, worship and teaching from the Scriptures. But there was a difference, and not only doctrinal; the new wine of the Holy Spirit had brought a vitality into the corporate gatherings. Jesus himself had said that new wine could not be contained in old wineskins. New wineskins have the flexibility to contain new wine. The old wineskins of Temple and synagogue, representing the Jewish religion, had to make way for new wineskins. Assemblies were formed that had the flexibility to allow for worship, prayer and ministry under the direction of the Holy Spirit.

Early church meetings

It is in the first epistle to the Corinthians that we gain most insight into the style of meetings of the early church. The Corinthians had become very preoccupied with spiritual gifts, particularly speaking in tongues. The freedom of the Spirit had given way to indiscipline in church gatherings. Speaking in tongues was disorderly and there seemed to be very little understanding of how a body should function, with all the spiritual gifts distributed for the common good. Paul gives some guidelines as to how the gifts should be exercised.

His desire is clearly to see a functioning, loving, spirit-filled meeting where each person is able to make their contribution. Both the prophetic and the priestly aspects of worship are implicit in 1 Corinthians 12-14—the prophetic by virtue of the emphasis on the gift of prophecy, and the priestly by virtue of the fact that all may minister, all have a function.

The directions for corporate worship are best summed up in 1 Corinthians 14:26—'What is the outcome then, brethren? When you assemble, each one has a psalm, has a teaching, has a revelation, has a tongue, has an interpretation. Let all things be done for edification.' This kind of meeting was a natural evolution from the synagogue. Two similar scriptures give a little insight into the nature of early Christian worship: Ephesians 5:18-19—'Be filled with the Spirit, speaking to one another in psalms and hymns and spiritual songs, singing and making melody with your heart to the Lord.' And Colossians 3:16—'Let the word of Christ richly dwell within you, with all wisdom, teaching and admonishing one another with psalms and hymns and spiritual songs, singing with thankfulness in your hearts to God.'

The emphasis in these three passages of Scripture is on participation, revelation (either through spiritual gifts or teaching) and edification. F. F. Bruce in *The Spreading Flame*, commenting on the early church at worship, says,

> The joy and exultation of these early days found expression in praises to God. For their praises the primitive Christians had the Old Testament Book of Psalms ready to hand, and in several of these Psalms they found adumbrations of the advent and work of the Messiah.
>
> But the reference to 'spiritual songs' in the New Testament epistles suggests that many Christians found a new song in their mouths, springing up spontaneously by the power of the Spirit of Christ within them.[5]

From these scriptures (1 Cor 12-14; Col 3:16; Eph 5:18-19) we can surmise that the early church's gatherings were based on the synagogue style of worship, with an emphasis on the exposition of Scripture, but with the added dimension of the Holy Spirit bringing life and creativity, distributing gifts and ministries, with each member of the congregation being free to participate within the discipline and order outlined by Paul.

Psalms, hymns, spiritual songs and singing by the Spirit were integral ingredients in the dynamic of the early church gatherings. The Old Testament book of Psalms provided a rich inheritance of songs for the early church. The Hebrew title for the book of Psalms was *Tehillim*, meaning 'songs of praise'. (For a fuller understanding of *Tehillim*, turn to Appendix 1.)

The word 'psalm' comes from the Greek *psalmos* which literally means 'the twitching of the fingers over the strings of a musical instrument'. The book of Psalms is a collection of songs which in their original format would have been accompanied by musical instruments. Converts from Judaism would have known the Psalms and would have easily adapted them for Christian worship. Gentile believers did not have the same heritage, but under the inspiration of the Holy Spirit were able to compose songs in the manner of the psalms, and so Paul is referring here to something beyond just singing from the Old Testament Psalter. It would have been the practice of the early church to bring a psalm from the word, and also a psalm from the Spirit.

The word 'hymn' comes from the Greek *hymnos*, meaning a song of praise to the gods. These songs were performed chorally. A New Testament hymn would be a song composed in praise of God. There are various passages of the New Testament which many scholars believe are fragments of hymns. Ephesians 5:14—'Awake, sleeper, and arise from the dead, and Christ will shine on you'—was thought to be an early baptismal hymn. 1 Timothy 3:16 is another example: 'He who was revealed in the flesh, was vindicated in the Spirit, beheld by angels, proclaimed among the nations, believed on in the world, taken up in glory.'

Spiritual songs would have been songs with a Christian content. Songs, or odes, were lyrical verses set to music and could be about a wide range of subjects. The implication is that songs about the Christian life could be used in the church gathering, as they are inspired by the Holy Spirit.

Psalms, hymns and spiritual songs speak of a variety of ways of bringing praise and worship to God. In those early gatherings not only was God exalted through singing, but instruction, teaching and even admonition were brought through the singing of psalms, hymns and spiritual songs.

Another form of singing mentioned by Paul is found in 1 Corinthians 14:15—'I shall sing with the spirit and I shall sing with the mind also.' Paul had just been reasoning about speaking in tongues and how the gift is to be properly used. He says, 'For if I pray in a tongue, my spirit prays, but my mind is unfruitful.' In the very next verse he says, 'I shall pray with the spirit and I shall pray with the mind also,' suggesting that there is a time to pray in tongues, as well as a time to pray in his normal language. His very next statement suggests the same can apply to singing: 'I shall sing with the spirit and I shall sing with the mind also.' The context and logic of the argument is that there is a time to sing in normal language (psalms, hymns, spiritual songs) where the mind is involved. There is also a time to sing in tongues, to 'sing with the spirit'.

The grammatical construction of the expression, 'I will sing with the spirit' is dative of instrument which expresses cause or manner. So either the spirit is the cause of the singing, or the manner of the singing is by the spirit. Either way, the suggestion is that there is a type of singing in which our spirits are active, responding to the Holy Spirit. In a sermon preached at Westminster Chapel and appearing in the *Westminster Record* Vol. 43, no. 2, Dr Martyn Lloyd-Jones, commenting on this particular passage, says:

> What do you think the Apostle sang? What was he singing, do you think, when he says he sang with the spirit? Well, he is referring to being in a state of ecstasy in which, under the inspiration

and impulse, and movement and guidance of the Spirit, he is
giving utterance to things he had never contemplated before. As
men spoke in tongues so they sang like this in the spirit. He is *not*
talking about singing psalms. When you sing the psalms of the
Old Testament you do not do so under the immediate inspiration
of the Spirit, you do so with understanding. But there is this kind
of spiritual ecstatic singing.

The essential point that Dr Lloyd-Jones is making is that
speaking and singing in tongues existed in the early church.
However, speaking and singing in tongues does not necessarily imply a state of ecstasy. The Holy Spirit imparts the
ability to speak and sing in tongues, but the will is involved in
the exercise of that ability.

There can be no doubt that the early church was a singing,
praising, worshipping church. Under the influence of the Holy
Spirit, those early gatherings would have been in a truly
charismatic dimension. Psalms of praise, hymns, spiritual
songs, both composed and spontaneous, singing in tongues,
all were means of expressing the new song that God had put in
the hearts of the new Christians.

Prophetic utterances, tongues and interpretations, words of
wisdom and knowledge, healings, exhortations, discerning of
spirits, miracles, acts of faith, giving money, as well as the
exposition and teaching of Scripture, were some of the ways in
which individuals could contribute to the meetings. It would
be hard to imagine that the singing of psalms would have been
formal and lifeless. The Psalms express a whole variety of
ways in which praise and worship can be brought to God:
'Bless the Lord', 'Give thanks', 'Praise the Lord', 'Magnify
His Name', 'Sing to the Lord', 'Shout to God', 'Shout joyfully
with psalms', 'Clap your hands', 'Lift up your hands', 'Dance',
'Bow down', 'Kneel', 'Worship', 'Praise the Lord with
instruments'.

It would appear from the writings of Paul that the infant
church was charismatic in its variety of ministries and creative
in its worship. We do not know what the worship sounded
like, but we can assume that the life and joy of spirit-filled

lives gave full vent to that joy in the kind of expressions of worship and praise contained in the Psalms. We may dare to conjecture that among the exercise of the ministries which are more clearly described, there would have been corporate singing, hand-clapping, dancing, shouting, hand-raising, kneeling and bowing, all deriving from the original directives in the Psalms.

The post-apostolic period

After the death of the original apostles, the next 200 years furnish us with very little information regarding how the church worshipped. There is more emphasis on descriptions of the community lifestyle and the form of the gatherings than on the style of singing and music. Justin Martyr, writing in the second century, describes a typical church meeting:

> At the end of the prayers, we salute one another with a kiss. There is then brought to the president of the brethren, bread and a cup of wine mixed with water; and he taking them up offers up praise and glory to the Father of the universe through the name of the Son and of the Holy Ghost, and gives thanks at considerable length for our being counted worthy to receive these things at His hands. When he has concluded the prayers and thanksgivings, all the people present express their joyful assent by saying Amen. And when the president has given thanks, and all the people have expressed their joyful assent, those who are called by us as deacons give to each of those present to partake of the bread and wine.[6]

We do not know if the absence of any mention of music is because the singing of the former years had now died out, or that it was there but just not mentioned. We do know that during the next 200 years there were various hymn writers. Around the year 112, Pliny the Younger recorded that the Christians had a custom of singing hymns to Christ.

In his book *From Christ to Constantine*, M. A. Smith analyses worship and church life in the third century:

The doorkeepers admitted the worshippers and often men and women were segregated on opposite sides of the church. The service would divide into two parts, the preaching and the Bible reading coming first, followed by the eucharist. Assistant clergy would read the lessons and conduct the prayers. The prayers would still be extempore, but their form and content would be fairly predictable. We have samples of prayers from this period on papyrus from Egypt, which bear every sign of having been written down for a particular occasion—congregational hymn singing was unknown as yet, but there might be solo singing, if a suitably gifted person was a member of the congregation.[7]

It would appear that Paul's injunction to the Corinthians, Ephesians and Colossians had been forgotten by the third century. However, some hymns were written during the period between the death of the first apostles and Constantine. In 1896 a papyrus was found in the Egyptian town of Oxyrhynchos containing the fragment of a hymn written towards the end of the third century. Written in musical notation, the influence of the Greeks could definitely be detected.

Some hymn writers used the medium of verse and music to counteract various heresies. In the second century Clement of Alexandria wrote hymns, and in the fourth century Chrysostom and Ephraim both used hymn writing as a means of communicating sound doctrine. During the fourth century Ambrose, the Bishop of Milan, popularized hymn singing. He appears to have been a very saintly man who took his ministry seriously. When he baptized Augustine, 'according to legend the two spontaneously improvised the Te Deum in alternate verses. This legend is thought to refer to what was undoubtedly a practice in the early church, namely the creation of hymns under the inspiration of strong religious feeling, somewhat the way today new phrases of text and new melodic variations spontaneously arise during the enthusiasm of a camp meeting.'[8]

It appears that after the age of psalms, hymns, spiritual songs, and spontaneous, spirit-led singing that there was a decline in the kind of worship and body life that Paul had described. There were exceptions, but the church was a long way from the dynamic of the earlier years.

Christian music became fossilized into an art form with a liturgy so inflexible that there was no room for the inspiration and creativity of the Holy Spirit. As scholars learned to write in musical notation, the chant became an established part of the liturgy of the church. Pope Gregory is said to have received chants from the Holy Spirit which his scribes then wrote down. A tradition of liturgical church music was born which has affected both the established church and the history of music. How quickly man imposed his own intellect and wisdom onto the creative and extemporaneous nature of worship in the early church.

From the time of Gregory in the sixth century to Luther in the sixteenth, congregational participation in worship was absent. It would need the intervention of God himself to change what man had done with his church. Over the centuries there have been outpourings of the Holy Spirit in revival which have restored certain truths to the church. In all revivals there has been an emphasis on worship, and often this has included an emphasis on new music as a means of bringing psalms, hymns and spiritual songs to God.

Worship and revivals

The Reformation not only affected the church's doctrine, it also affected its worship. Luther was himself a skilled musician, and he reintroduced congregational participation in hymn singing. He determined to put God's word into people's mouths by writing songs in the language and music of ordinary people. He unashamedly borrowed German folk melodies, making his songs popular. The critics and enemies of Luther declared that he had done more harm to them by his songs than by his sermons. A popular Martin Luther hymn today is, 'A safe stronghold our God is still, a trusty shield and weapon.'

Following Luther, there has been a rich stream of evangelical hymn writers right up to the present day. In 1707 Isaac

Watts published a new hymn book called *Hymns and Spiritual Songs*. The title page of the first edition states that these hymns were collected from the Scriptures, composed on divine subjects, and prepared for the Lord's Supper. Watts also wrote an essay: 'Towards the improvement of Christian psalmody, by the use of evangelical hymns in worship, as well as the Psalms of David.' Isaac Watts could well be considered the father of the kind of hymn singing which has been a feature of church life in the last 300 years. Such hymns as 'Jesus shall reign' and 'When I survey the wondrous cross' have stood the test of time. His hymns are free from poetic sentimentality and are truly Christ conscious.

The great revival of the eighteenth century under Whitefield and Wesley produced many superb hymns. Charles Wesley's output of 6,000 hymns has surpassed anyone before or after him. E. H. Broadbent comments:

> Charles Wesley though not equal to his brother in ability as a preacher, fully shared his labours. His greatest and lasting service to the church is in the hymns he wrote; they exceed six thousand in number, and many of them are of a poetic beauty and a spiritual value which place them among the best that have ever been written. They contain in beautiful and arresting form sound expositions of many of the principal doctrines taught in scripture, and they express worship, and the inward experiences of the spirit in a way which make them continually suited to give utterance to the longings and praises of hearts touched by the Spirit of God. The Wesleys, finding that most people take their theology more from hymns than scripture, wrote hymns with the definite purpose of teaching doctrine by them.[9]

The Wesleys were thus fulfilling Paul's injunction to teach and admonish one another by means of psalms, hymns and spiritual songs.

There is a rich heritage of hymn writing in Wales. During the revival of 1904–6 there was a strong emphasis on worship. Congregations would spontaneously burst forth into singing, and different members of the congregation under the anointing of the Spirit would sing extemporaneously. In Eifion

Evans' gripping book on the Welsh revival we read about the nature of these meetings:

> The verse of the Welsh hymn 'The man who suffered under the nails for a sinful man like me' was repeated several times. Many of the congregation, in the ecstasy of their spiritual deliverance, were unable to restrain themselves from dancing without either inhibition or irreverence. At the young people's prayer meeting which followed, the noise of prayer (some dozen or so praying simultaneously), weeping and shouting was at once deafening and harmonious.[10]

W. T. Stead, a London journalist, came to Wales to report on the revival. His report reads:

> The meetings open—after any amount of preliminary singing, while the congregation is assembling—by the reading of a chapter or a psalm. Then it is go as you please for two hours or more. And the amazing thing is that it does go and does not get entangled in what might seem to be inevitable confusion. Three quarters of the meeting consists of singing. No one uses a hymn book. No one gives out a hymn. The last person to control the meeting in any way is Mr Evan Roberts (a leading figure in the revival). People pray and sing, give testimony; exhort as the Spirit moves them.[11]

This meeting sounds very similar to the kind of meeting described by Paul in 1 Corinthians 14.

There are other significant moves of God which have brought a new music with them. The evangelistic campaigns of D. L. Moody were enriched by the music of Ira Sankey, a soloist who wrote songs in a very popular style. The waltz was a popular contemporary dance at the time of the Moody campaigns, and Sankey made full use of the lilting three-four rhythms for many of his hymns. 'Master the tempest is raging' and 'Faith is the victory' can still be heard in many churchs today.

In 1865 the Salvation Army began an evangelistic thrust which took the gospel to over eighty nations. A strong emphasis on the music of the people, together with simple words expressing gospel truth, carried the message into the open air

with brass bands, colourful banners and uniforms, and a
spirit-filled joy that helped to bring a major spiritual and
social revolution to Victorian England.

We are now living in days with a rich heritage of evangelical, Spirit-inspired music. Over the last twenty years the
charismatic movement has released a whole new stream of
psalms, hymns and spiritual songs into the church. We have
seen that, since those early days of the church with its life,
vitality, creativity and participation in Spirit-led worship, that
there has been decline and neglect. Church music became
static and a greater emphasis was placed on the artistic aspect
rather than the spiritual.

At this point we need to recognize that the restoration of
worship is inextricably bound up with the restoration of the
structures of our churches. Some may start by looking at
structures and then realize the implications this has for worship. For others, probably the majority, the starting-point will
be a desire to see worship taking a lively and more prominent
part in church life. Questions will then need to be asked about
how churches are governed and the traditions upon which
their gatherings are based.

Baptism in the Spirit and personal renewal in worship can
only find full satisfaction in the context of a body of people
with similar experiences who desire to see the implications for
church life realized. Worship is both a personal and corporate
activity. Therefore, as the church restores what has been lost
in worship so it must also recover what has been lost in body
life in order for that worship to find full expression. The restoration of worship will inevitably be accompanied by the restoration of the anointed body of Christ.

3

The Anointed Body

With sandal-shod feet and ill-fitting robe, hair all unkempt and eyes aglow, the prophet stands in our imagination. Conditioned by storybook pictures, television and cinema epics, we formulate an image in our minds. Our prejudice breeds suspicion of anyone radical enough to challenge the status quo, be it political, social, scientific or religious, so we caricature and nervously laugh at the prophet and his message. An eccentric class who claim an ability to perceive and a right to challenge, they are not an everyday sort of people. And yet God made us to be prophets—and not only prophets but priests and kings as well.

Man's moral, intellectual, emotional and physical capacities were bestowed by God for a fulfilling and enriching relationship: 'As a prophet he was endowed with knowledge and understanding, as a priest he was endowed with righteousness and holiness. As a king he was given authority to rule over God's creation.'[12]

A joyful harmony existed between God and man. The carefree abandon of their relationship is expressed in Proverbs 8:30-31—'Then I was beside Him [wisdom], as a master workman; and I was daily His delight, rejoicing always before Him, rejoicing in the world, His earth, and having my delight in the sons of men.' Wisdom, personified as a master workman, rejoices in God's creation. The Hebrew word for rejoice as used here means to have sport, to play.

God's original intention was that man would be able to enjoy God in a complete relationship. *The Shorter Westminster Catechism* states that 'man's chief end is to glorify God, and enjoy Him forever'. Made in the image of God, and with the capacity to worship and adore, man's greatest fulfilment comes by giving full expression to thoughts and feelings that are directed towards the heavenly Father.

The tragedy of the fall deprived man of this loving, intimate relationship. The prophetic dimension was forfeited as darkness clouded the understanding and man became 'futile in his speculations' (Rom 1:21). Instead of robes of righteousness and holiness, the garments of guilt and shame clothed man with condemnation and fear. His priesthood now withdrawn, he could no longer minister to God. And neither could he rule: toil and sweat replaced a dignified kingly exercise of authority over God's creation. The fall wasted the prophetic, the priestly and the kingly in man.

With the gradual unfolding of the revelation of God's purpose for his people, contained in the Old Testament, there came the establishment of three ministries through which the people related to God. Each was anointed with oil, a beautiful and fragrant blend of liquid myrrh, cinnamon, cane, cassia and olive oil. This anointing symbolized the setting apart of these ministries by the Holy Spirit for their particular function.

The prophet's ministry was to hear from God and communicate his word to the people. Sometimes there would be encouragement, sometimes challenge, sometimes rebuke. Often called a seer because of his ability to see God's purpose, and sometimes called a gusher, bringing to mind a fountain of cascading water, the prophet's message would burst forth, an uncontainable torrent of words, directing God's people in the way they should go.

After the exodus from Egypt, God established the priesthood in the nation of Israel. His original intention was that the whole nation should be a 'kingdom of priests' (Ex 19:6). However, with this call came such a manifestation of God's presence on Mount Sinai that fear filled the people and only Aaron could approach God with Moses. Although God's purpose was that all should be priests, there was still a great gap between God and the people because of sin. God therefore instituted the priesthood through Aaron so that he could act as a mediator between God and the people. He was given special clothes to wear, symbolizing righteousness and holiness. He had to undergo a ceremonial washing, symbolizing cleansing from sin, and he was anointed with oil, separating him for his priestly function. Hebrews 5 explains the role and ministry of the priest. He is taken from men to represent them to God. He is appointed by God to act on men's behalf before him. He offers gifts and sacrifices and makes intercession. The Aaronic priesthood of the Old Testament thus enabled the people to come to God.

Israel was essentially a theocracy. God was her ruler and his rule was exercised through the prophets and priests. The time came when God allowed her to have a king and he was set apart, by anointing, to exercise rule and government on God's behalf. Saul was the first king, but his rule was disastrous. He started well, but through his disobedience he lost the kingdom. His life ended in suicide.

God re-established rule and government in David, 'a man after [God's] own heart' (1 Sam 13:14). With David's accession to the throne of Israel a new era of God's purpose was unveiled, speaking prophetically of the coming Messiah and the advent of the kingdom of God. It was in David that the three dimensions of serving God were combined. Anointed as king, he also wore the linen ephod of the priest, and had remarkable prophetic insights into God's purpose for the future. As an Old Testament king, priest and prophet he fulfilled God's original purpose for man in the way he related to God. There were, of course, many imperfections in him, and so he could not fully exemplify God's original intention for man. But as he exercised his kingly, prophetic and priestly ministries, he pointed the way to the one who embodied them perfectly—the Lord Jesus Christ.

God gave David special revelation about praise and worship. He wrote many psalms and was responsible for instituting a comprehensive and vital musical tradition, complete with instrumentalists and singers, as a means of giving full musical intepretation to the Psalms.

Many of the Psalms are expressions of praise and worship in the three dimensions in which we can relate to God, the kingly, the prophetic and the priestly. The prophetic element in the Psalms declares the greatness of God's character and his purposes in establishing the kingdom. There is a prophetic note which points to the kingdom reaching the ends of the earth:

> Sing to God, O kingdoms of the earth; sing praises to the Lord, to Him who rides upon the highest heavens, which are from ancient times; behold, he speaks forth with his voice, a mighty voice. Ascribe strength to God; His majesty is over Israel, and His strength is in the skies. O God, Thou art awesome from Thy sanctuary (Ps 68:32-35).

This call to the kingdoms of the earth to sing praises to God would have gone beyond the understanding of Israel at that time. It is a prophetic voice, proclaiming the power of the gospel to reach the ends of the earth, and is a recurring theme in the Psalms (Pss 2:8-9; 8; 22:27; 86:9). A further prophetic element in the Psalms points to the coming of Jesus. Psalms 2, 18 and 110, for example, proclaim his kingly, prophetic and priestly ministries.

The reign of David was distinguished by its worship. Worship which proclaimed the character of God, declaring his ways and intentions. Worship where spiritual sacrifice, the sacrifice of praise, was offered by a ministering priesthood. Worship which, by its very proclamation, executed the authority and rule of God:

Let the high praises of God be in their mouth, and a two-edged sword in their hand, to execute vengeance on the nations, and punishment on the peoples; to bind their kings with chains, and their nobles with fetters of iron; to execute on them the judgment written; This is an honour for *all* His godly ones (Ps 149:6-9, my italics).

All that David's reign foreshadowed became substance in the coming of Jesus. When Jesus began his public ministry in Nazareth, he declared that he was the fulfilment of Isaiah's prophecy:

The Spirit of the Lord is upon Me, because He has anointed Me to preach the gospel to the poor. He has sent Me to proclaim release to the captives, and recovery of sight to the blind, to set free those who are downtrodden, to proclaim the favourable year of the Lord (Lk 4:18-19).

Jesus was anointed, not with oil, but with the Holy Spirit. His ministry was to establish a kingdom where he was the king. He would do this by declaring the word of God prophetically, both by his life and his message. Before the kingdom could be established there was a battle to be won. Jesus, the great High Priest, offered up to the Father the sacrifice of his own life, thus defeating Satan on behalf of his people.

Jesus, the second Adam, came as prophet, priest and king —three dimensions in which he related to his Father. He was the word made flesh—he articulated in himself the message of God to the human race—the supreme prophet. He exercised kingly rule and authority—demons, disease, even the elements were subject to his authority. He proclaimed a kingdom unfettered by geographical boundaries.

As priest, Jesus represented man to God and God to man. He interceded for his disciples. He sacrificed his life to reconcile us to God:

For it was fitting that we should have such a high priest, holy, innocent, undefiled, separated from sinners and exalted above the heavens; who does not need daily, like those high priests, to offer up sacrifices, first for His own sins, and then for the sins of the people, because this He did once for all when He offered up Himself (Heb 7:26-27).

It is, therefore, through the anointed Lord Jesus that we are reconciled to God and have restored to us the prophetic, priestly and kingly dimensions of our lives. Moreover, they are restored to a greater measure than Adam enjoyed. Isaac Watts pithily expresses our position: 'In Him the tribes of Adam boast more blessings than their father lost.'

An anointed people

God has restored the prophetic, priestly and kingly dimensions to us, but his purpose is greater than our individual and personal restoration. God desires an anointed people, a royal priesthood, a kingdom of priests to our God, a people who by their lifestyle and testimony are a prophetic voice to the world. Just as Jesus was anointed with the Spirit to be prophet, priest and king, so the body of Christ can live and move in the same anointing, functioning corporately in these dimensions.

Peter's description of the church reveals God's intention for a corporate people: 'But you are a chosen race, a royal priesthood, a holy nation, a people for God's own possession, that you may proclaim the excellences of Him who has called you out of darkness into His marvellous light' (1 Pet 2:9).

The people of God are to be a priesthood. Washed and cleansed through the blood of Jesus, and clothed in his righteousness, we present ourselves as living sacrifices to God. We minister to him as we bring the sacrifice of praise. We are able to make priestly intercession for others as we come to God on their behalf. When we enter into praise together, we are functioning as a priesthood.

The prophetic nature of God's people is displayed by their ability to speak out God's word. Worship, evangelism, fellowship, the exercise of spiritual gifts, preaching and practical acts of service all communicate truths about God, and in this sense they are all prophetic.

As citizens of the kingdom we have executive authority to implement the decrees of the kingdom, the truths contained in God's word. We do this when we pray according to the will of God and proclaim the word of God in our worship. Jesus proclaimed liberty to the captives. We have authority to liberate captives, and when in faith we speak what God says into captive situations, we are being both prophetic and kingly. Acts of faith which defy the natural order of things, such as healing the sick and casting out demons, are the enforcing of the kingdom. We not only pray, 'Thy Kingdom come', but we act in a manner which gives credibility to our prayer.

An understanding of the church as an anointed body with a prophetic, priestly and ruling function, a people who have been called out of darkness to declare the praises of God, should radically affect our desire for worship, the way we worship, and our expectation in worship. God has made us prophets, priests and kings so that loving him, sharing our lives with him, and enjoying his presence is gloriously possible.

4

Prophetic Worship

Even amidst great blessing, with the church expanding daily, controversy raged. Should the new gentile Christians be subjected to the law of Moses and, in particular, should they be circumcised? Some taught that observance of the law and circumcision were conditional to salvation.

Paul and Barnabas had just returned from a successful missionary outreach. Their home church at Antioch thrilled to the details of how a door of faith had been opened to the gentiles and many had been saved. But when some men from Judea arrived in Antioch to teach, their understanding of the gospel was different from that of Paul and Barnabas. Debate and discussion ensued.

It was decided that such an important issue should be discussed by the apostles and elders in the Jerusalem church. When Paul and Barnabas arrived in Jerusalem they reported all that God had been doing. The problem of circumcision again raised its head as some believing Pharisees began to argue for keeping the law of Moses. The council of apostles and elders was formed to discuss this vital issue of doctrine. James, the leading brother of the Jerusalem church, was the chairman of the meeting. Peter, Paul and Barnabas all related their experiences of God's working in signs and wonders among the gentiles.

The doctrinal issue, when it was resolved, would set a vital precedent for understanding the nature of salvation. It is a doctrine so vital that Paul wrote a whole epistle explaining it; a doctrine which permeated all his writings and would certainly have been an integral part of his teachings: the doctrine of salvation by grace alone. Law, whether the law of Moses or any other imposed rule or regulation, cannot achieve righteousness.

Several years later when Paul wrote to the believers in Philippi, he said, 'For it is we who are the circumcision, we who worship by the Spirit of God, who glory in Christ Jesus, and who put no confidence in the flesh' (Phil 3:3, New International Version). A new covenant had superceded the old. Rituals and laws, with their rigorous demands, had been replaced by the laws of God lovingly written on the hearts of those whom God had chosen for eternal life. The initiative was God's. Grace meant that Jew and gentile alike, in their total incapacity to find favour with God, had both found a way through to his redeeming grace.

James, in summing up the discussion of the council, quoted from the prophet Amos, stressing the fulfilment of God's purpose for the gentiles:

> After these things I will return, and I will rebuild the tabernacle of David which has fallen, and I will rebuild its ruins, and I will restore it, in order that the rest of mankind may seek the Lord, and all the Gentiles who are called by My name, says the Lord, who makes these things known from of old (Acts 15:16-18).

Thousands of years earlier God had made a covenant with Abraham, telling him that through his seed all nations of the earth would be blessed (Gen 17). God's purpose from the beginning has been to have a people for himself drawn from every tribe and tongue and nation. In his epistle to the Romans, Paul outlines the condition by which this promise would be fulfilled:

For the promise to Abraham or to his descendants that he would
be heir of the world was not through the Law, but through the
righteousness of faith . . . For this reason it is by faith, that it
might be in accordance with grace, in order that the promise may
be certain to all the descendants, not only to those who are of the
Law [Jews], but also to those who are of the faith of Abraham,
who is the father of us all (Rom 4:13, 16).

God's promise of nations to Abraham is a theme which runs
through many of the prophetic writings. Isaiah and Jeremiah
both saw ahead to days when a new covenant would supercede the old and God's plan and purpose would go beyond the
Jewish race to include the blessing of all nations.

Amos, like many of the prophets, challenged the sinfulness
of his day and warned Israel of impending judgement. The
warning was not heeded, ending in seventy years of captivity.
He also promised restoration and forgiveness, and a blessing
upon the gentile nations (Amos 9:12). After the seventy years
of exile, the captive Jews migrated back to Israel. The walls of
the city were rebuilt and the Temple was restored.

The prophets had certainly foretold a time of restoration,
but the extravagant language and imagery used in their descriptions went far beyond the reality of what happened his-
torically (e.g. Is 58-66). The Temple was never restored to the
former glory of Solomon, and there was no sense of the super-
natural presence of God. The shekinah glory which had
hovered over the ark of the covenant in the Holy of Holies
during the great days of Solomon was absent. The high priest
was no longer able to communicate with God. The next 400
years would be a time of spiritual poverty, with the prophetic
voice silent.

The prophecies concerning restoration were pointing beyond the immediate historical fulfilment to a new age, a new
covenant. They were indicating the coming of Jesus and the
establishing of his kingdom. It would be in the new covenant
age that God's promise to Abraham would be fulfilled.

Amos' prophecy of the restoration of God's people had
much broader implications than the return from the Baby-

lonian captivity. He foresaw a time when the gentile nations
would own the name of God (Amos 9:11-12). The fact that
James took the promise of Amos and applied it to the church
shows the spiritual nature of its fulfilment. James is using the
prophecy to justify the coming in of the gentiles, the fulfilling
of God's promise. He could have chosen many prophetic
scriptures to make his point, but the Holy Spirit particularly
guided him to this one. A significant factor in bringing in the
gentiles would be the restoration of David's Tabernacle which
had fallen.

The Tabernacle of David

To understand the Tabernacle of David we need first of all to
understand the Tabernacle of Moses. During the forty years
in the wilderness, God gave Moses detailed instructions to
erect a tent (or tabernacle). The Hebrew word translated
'tabernacle' simply means a dwelling-place. The Tabernacle
was to be a place where God would manifest his presence.
There was an outer section and then an inner section called
the Holy of Holies. This was to contain an intricately designed
box, overlaid with gold, having two cherubim carved in gold
on each side. Inside this box, called the ark of the covenant,
were the two tablets of stone on which were inscribed the ten
commandments; some manna, the food which God supplied
to sustain them in the wilderness; and Aaron's rod which had
budded supernaturally. It was in the Holy of Holies that the
shekinah glory, God's manifest presence, would hover. Only
the high priest was allowed into the Holy of Holies, once a
year on the Day of Atonement, and then only after an elaborate process of blood sacrifice. The Tabernacle became the
focal point for the spiritual life of Israel. The tent of meeting
represented the dwelling-place of God.

When the Israelites entered the promised land, the Tabernacle was established at Shiloh. After a time of backsliding,
the Philistines devastated the Tabernacle and stole the ark of
the covenant. With various calamities befalling them because

of the presence of the ark, the Philistines released it and it came back to Israel to the home of Abinadab in Kiriath-jearim where it remained for twenty years.

When David became king of Israel he desired to bring the ark into Jerusalem, having established that city as the capital. There was an abortive attempt to remove the ark, which failed because of disobedience over God's instructions for transporting it, but eventually it was brought into Jerusalem.

The procession of the ark into the city must have been a remarkable occasion. The Levites carried it in the prescribed manner, while musicians and singers rejoiced before God with singing and dancing. Chief musicians were appointed to lead the instruments and singing. David himself danced with all his might. 'All Israel brought up the ark of the covenant of the Lord with shouting, and with sound of the horn, with trumpets, with loud-sounding cymbals, with harps and lyres' (1 Chron 15:28). Thus began a new era in the life of Israel. David was given a special revelation about praise and worship. It was a time of creativity, of music and dancing, of singing and rejoicing. It was an age of accomplishment in establishing Israel as a great nation.

While the ark was installed on Mount Zion, the old Tabernacle, minus the ark of the covenant, was established on Mount Gibeon. Mount Gibeon was the place where the old Mosaic laws and commands for sacrifice were observed, whereas on Mount Zion there was freedom and simplicity in approaching the ark. It is a remarkable picture of law and grace. Gibeon represented the old way, while at the Tabernacle of David on Mount Zion there was an Old Testament glimpse of new covenant life.

During the dark days that followed David's reign, Amos the Prophet declared that a day was coming when the Tabernacle of David would be restored. He looked forward to a day of grace, of new covenant life, of freedom of approach to God without the ritual of blood sacrifice. No wonder James, in justifying a gospel of grace free from the Mosaic law, refers to the restoration of David's Tabernacle with its freedom, simplicity and vitality.

The musical life at David's Tabernacle

With the setting up of David's Tabernacle came a new order of praise and worship. David gave instructions to the Levites which allowed for spontaneous, joyful celebration interwoven with a sense of God's order, everything being done according to the commandment of David.

Chenaniah, the chief of the Levites, was in charge of the singing because he was skilful. The singers, Heman, Asaph and Ethan, were appointed to sound aloud on cymbals of bronze. There were harps tuned in the upper register, called the alamoth, and lyres tuned to the sheminith. These were harps with the strings tuned an octave apart, giving a full and sonorous sound. The sheminith and alamoth tunings would have giving a broad depth to the sound of the musical accompaniment as they combined with the cymbals, raising sounds of joy to the singing led by Chenaniah, the chief musician.

After the ark had been installed on Mount Zion, the spiritual life of the nation became focused on David's Tabernacle. Instead of the sacrificial ritual of the Tabernacle of Moses, there was free access into the Holy of Holies, the ark being on view for all to see. This was a tabernacle of grace prefiguring the new covenant where we all, as a royal priesthood, have free entrance to God through the new and living way by the blood of Jesus. The main characteristic of this tabernacle was that it was surrounded by joyful worship with a great release of prophesying with musical instruments.

The first book of Chronicles gives full details of the musical life of the Tabernacle of David, revealing the structure and order for the musicians and singers. Instruments had a prominent part and would have accompanied the singing.

There were 4,000 Levites who were appointed to play and sing day and night so the praise before the ark was continuous. There appears to be a musical hierarchy according to David's appointment. Chenaniah was the master of singing, but Asaph, Heman and Jeduthun also had a leading role to teach and train their sons (1 Chron 25). These three had twenty four sons between them, and they in turn led the twenty-four courses (or groves) of musicians from their relatives, making a group of 288 musicians trained and skilful in singing, playing instruments and prophesying. Thus from the skill and expertise of a group of well-trained musicians the whole musical life of the nation was affected. Chenaniah, under King David's direction, would have overseen everything. Asaph, Heman and Jeduthun would have given their sons special training which would then have been passed on to their relatives. Eventually all the families would have learned how to make music before the Lord.

When the whole congregation of Israel gathered before the ark, there would have been the opportunity for everyone to participate in the praise and worship. It was not that these trained prophetic musicians would give a performance, but the music and words God had given them would have carried the congregation with them. Could it be that as God gave David a psalm, he would teach it to Chenaniah, who would then gather around him the chief musicians? Perhaps as they were taking the words of David, the Spirit of God would move on them, and they would begin to prophesy one to another with musical accompaniment (1 Chron 25: 1-3). There could then be a response as another group would prophesy in giving thanks and praising the Lord for what had been said. As the words and melodies became a means of communicating God's prophetic message, they would have then passed on to their sons what they had learned. With the 288 in the 24 courses taking hold of the words, melodies and accompaniment, they could then encourage the whole congregation to participate in a glorious act of celebration and worship.

The congregation could participate by raising their hands, bursting into joyful applause, dancing, kneeling, lying prostrate before God, joining in a repetitive refrain, and fulfilling the many and varied injunctions to worship God. Thus a psalm, without the use of P.A., chorus books or overhead projectors, would have been ministered to the Lord with the whole congregation able to participate.

Sometimes in the psalm there would be a 'selah'. Thirty-nine of the Psalms have the word 'selah', twenty-eight of which give musical directions in their inscription. Although there is some vagueness about the exact meaning of the word, there is strong evidence to suggest that it was a musical inter-lude. The musicians would pick up the mood of what had been expressed and illustrate it musically. This would then give the congregation opportunity to meditate on the words and ask God for understanding. Music is a very powerful means of communication and selahs, when they are played skilfully by anointed musicians, can help a congregation to respond in their hearts to God. The use of the word 'selah' in the Psalms suggests that the music played expressed different moods. So the selah in Psalm 55, where the psalmist is expressing his desire for escape and to find refuge, would have very different musical content from the triumphant note of the selah in Psalm 49.

Form or Spirit?

In referring to the restoration of David's Tabernacle being fulfilled in the church, we need to understand the implications this has for worship in the new covenant. Can we transfer the style of Old Testament worship into the church, or is that pushing James's use of the Amos passage too far?

It is important to remember that the context of James' quotation of Amos is a discussion about the grace of God in salvation. Although he is not primarily talking about worship, it would seem logical that an understanding of grace will affect how we worship. James would have had an understanding of the Tabernacle of David and how it related to worship. In fact the worship in the Temple, and even to a small extent in the synagogue, had its roots in Davidic worship. As the church is the fulfilment of the Scripture regarding the restoration of David's Tabernacle, then the spirit and form of Davidic worship is relevant to the way we worship today.

Worship at the Tabernacle of David had a strong prophetic content. The Psalms are not only subjective poems dealing with the Psalmist's personal walk with God, but many of them contain great prophetic statements about the rule of God over the nations, the coming of the Messiah, and the establishing of God's kingdom on the earth. When the ark was taken into Jerusalem the musicians and singers declared:

> Oh give thanks to the Lord, call upon His Name;
>> Make known His deeds among the peoples.
> Sing to Him, sing praises to Him;
>> Speak of all his wonders.
> Glory in His holy name . . . .
>> Tell of His glory among the nations . . .
> For He is coming to judge the earth.
>> O give thanks to the Lord, for He is good:
>> For His loving kindness is everlasting.
>> Then say, 'Save us, O God of our salvation,
>> And gather us and deliver us from the nations,
>> To give thanks to Thy holy name,
> And glory in Thy praise'. (1 Chron 16:8-10, 24, 33-35).

In the book of Psalms God's salvation in the nations is a recurrent theme. The essence of Davidic worship was love for the God whose purpose was to reveal his glory among all the nations of the earth who would bring him worship. Love songs, intercessory heart cries, proclamations of faith, declarations of God's purpose, exhortations and expressions of heart-felt worship are all combined in the book of Psalms. When we bring a psalm in our worship we are fulfilling the prophetic word. The church today is being restored. Psalms from the Spirit and the word are still declaring the purposes and ways of God, just as they did in David's day.

The form, as well as the spirit, of Davidic worship is also being restored to the church today: the raising of hands, dance, corporate singing, kneeling, joyful shouting, hand-clapping, lying prostrate, and speaking truth, accompanied by musical instruments raising sounds of joy and playing appropriately to the words that are being expressed.

In the book of Revelation, John had a vision of the worship in heaven. There is a close link between the worship described in Revelation and the worship at David's Tabernacle. In David's Tabernacle there were twenty-four courses of musicians. In Revelation there are twenty-four elders with harps who lead the worship in heaven as they sing: 'Worthy art Thou to take the book, and to break its seals; for Thou wast slain, and didst purchase for God with Thy blood men from every tribe and tongue and people and nation. And Thou hast made them to be a kingdom and priests to our God; and they will reign upon the earth' (Rev 5:9-10).

Ralph Martin makes the following comment on worship in Revelation:

> The praise they offer (in the Book of Revelation) is to the holy and righteous God of Judaism who is extolled (as we have seen earlier) in the synagogue Liturgy as Creator and Sustainer of the world, and Judge of all. The introductory phrases which the seer of Revelation uses are interesting. The verses are prefaced by such terms as: 'they never ceased to sing'; 'singing'; 'the elders fell down on their faces and worshipped God, saying'; 'he said with a loud voice'; 'they sing the song of Moses'.
>
> All this suggests that the writer, the seer John whom Christian tradition names as 'the liturgist', sought to set forth his depictions of the heavenly scene and the celestial worship by projecting on to his canvas the forms and patterns which belonged to his knowledge of the worship of the Church on earth. For this feature there is a precedent, for it is known that later Judaism was familiar with the idea of the inter-relation of heavenly and earthly cultus. There are texts which speak of liturgical songs in heaven, but the language belongs to Jewish worship on the earth. It is certainly understandable that the Christian seer should resort to this practice of using the forms and cadre which were taken from his own experience. How else could he have made his descriptions intelligible to his readers?

Ralph Martin's suggestion is that John's aural revelation was based on what he had heard in the church. We do not know what worship at the Tabernacle of David sounded like, or what worship in the early church sounded like, but we do know that all joined in, that there were instruments, antiphonal responsive singing, shouting, and that the sound of singing was like the sound of a thunderous waterfall. The music of synagogue and Temple had its roots in the worship and music of David's Tabernacle. The early church's worship grew out of the synagogue and Temple worship.

God's plan for the church is that it should be a praising, worshipping community, thus individually and corporately obeying the first commandment. God is a creative God who has given us a wide range of expressions through which we can worship him. Prophetic worship in the New Testament is redolent with the atmosphere of the Tabernacle of David. It is worship as God intended it to be, not based on an inflexible ecclesiastical or liturgical tradition, but overflowing with the freshness and vitality of the Holy Spirit giving life to God's revelation in the Scriptures as to how we worship.

Many of the Psalms declare the sovereignty of God over all the earth, looking forward to the time when the King will be visible throughout all nations. The restoration of David's Tabernacle means that the prophetic vision contained in many of the Psalms written during David's era is being fulfilled in the age of the church:

> I will give Thee thanks with all my heart;
>> I will sing praises to Thee before the gods.
> I will bow down toward Thy holy temple,
>> And give thanks to Thy name for Thy loving kindness and Thy truth;
>> For Thou hast magnified Thy word according to All Thy name.
>> On the day I called Thou didst answer me;
> Thou didst make me bold with strength in my soul.
>> All the kings of the earth will give thanks to Thee, O Lord,
>> When they have heard the words of Thy mouth.
> And they will sing of the ways of the Lord.
>> For great is the glory of the Lord (Ps 138:1-5).

Under the new covenant we who have received grace can

worship, clothed in the righteousness of Christ, without fear or condemnation, knowing that a God who delights in his people gladly receives every creative expression of love towards him.

The prophetic fulfilment of the restoration of David's Tabernacle can be seen in the church. 'I will return' speaks of God's presence with his people. Just as the shekinah glory hovered over the Tabernacle, so now God's dwelling is in the midst of his people, the church, who are 'being built together into a dwelling of God in the Spirit' (Eph 2:22). The purpose of restoration is that through the church being built together into a worshipping and praising people, 'the rest of mankind may seek the Lord, and all the Gentiles who are called by My name, says the Lord who makes these things known from of old' (Acts 15:17-18).

5

In Spirit and in Truth

To the casual onlooker, the sparkling blue of the Aegean would have appeared inviting. To me the sight of land was a relief. After a day of cruising around some of the Greek islands in a small boat on a less than peaceful sea, the thought of standing on terra firma was becoming more attractive as the coastline of the mainland came into sharper focus. The islands were beautiful, the sea trip forgettable. That is until we approached the harbour of Piraeus. I suddenly forgot about my slight queasiness, and allowed my imagination to travel back 2,000 years.

The temples I saw covering the hillside, though now in ruins, were the same temples Paul would have seen when he sailed into Piraeus. But as I looked, my romantic dreaming turned to thoughts of what Paul did when he arrived in Athens. Standing on Mars Hill, he challenged the whole of Athens' cultural and religious life as he proclaimed the resurrection of Jesus. The statue dedicated to the unknown god gave Paul the introduction he needed to preach about Jesus. His sermon opened by identifying a basic need in man. The evidence for this need was scattered all over the hills of Greece. The need to worship. For the sophisticated Greeks and for the more primitive visitors from the tribes and nations that surrounded them, the worship of various gods was an essential part of life.

Originally, God placed within mankind a capacity for worship. In his state of rebellion, man sought to fill that vacuum with anything other than God himself. Rather than worship the living God who had revealed himself, mankind chose not to acknowledge or give thanks to him. The corruption of the human race which has turned its back on God is vividly described by Paul in Romans 1:20-23:

> For since the creation of the world [God's] invisible attributes, His eternal power and divine nature have been clearly seen, being understood through what has been made, so that they are without excuse. For even though they knew God, they did not honour him as God, or gave thanks; but they became futile in their speculations, and their foolish heart was darkened. Professing to be wise, they became fools, and exchanged the glory of the incorruptible God for an image in the form of corruptible man and of birds and four-footed animals and crawling creatures.

There is a basic awareness in man which tells him that he needs to find identity in something beyond himself. Primitive peoples turned to the sun, the moon, the wind and the rain in worship, hoping to find favour with the powers behind the elements on which they were dependent for their livelihood. Idols were made, identifying and personifying these various powers. Rituals, ceremonies and sacrificial rites of appeasement developed as primitive people expressed their commitment to their imagined gods. Great civilizations were built up around their concepts of various deities.

The Greeks and Romans worshipped various gods and named such planets as Jupiter, Mercury and Mars after them. The Romans deified Caesar, while the earlier Philistines worshipped an idol called Dagon. The Bible gives other examples of idol worship. In the promised land the Israelites were constantly tempted to worship Baal, and in the New Testament, Paul and Barnabas—much to their distress—were hailed at Lystra as messengers of Mercury after they had performed a miracle in the name of Jesus. In Ephesus the gospel created a violent reaction in those whose commercial interests were bound up with the goddess Artemis of the Ephesians. From the Aztecs to the Aborigines, from the Britons to the Babylonians, the worship of some form of deity constituted a normal part of life.

Idols personifying these various deities lacked any intrinsic power. Psalm 135, in mocking tone, compares the idols of the nations with the God of Israel:

> The idols of the nations are but silver and gold, the work of man's hands. They have mouths, but they do not speak; they have eyes, but they do not see; they have ears, but they do not hear; nor is there any breath at all in their mouth. Those who make them will be like them, yes, everyone who trusts in them.

Although the idols did not have any power in themselves, the priests, witch-doctors and other cultic leaders did wield power and authority. They did this by the manipulation of their gullible and fearful followers, and by drawing on occult powers, often with dreadful and awesome manifestations. The magicians of Egypt, by their black arts, were able to copy at least some of the miracles Moses was able to perform. Psychic powers, the ability to commune with departed spirits, to place curses, and even heal the sick, were all connected with the worship of idols. Idolatry touched the invisible world.

In our modern world we are not likely to make idols to bow down to, but man's rebellion towards God remains. His spiritual vacuum still needs to be filled, and so, whether consciously or unconsciously, man cannot help but be a worshipper. At base, humanism is the unconscious deification of man. This philosophy has so affected the thinking and values in education and politics that godly values have been undermined and Christian values are only deemed relevant if they do not contradict man's ideas. In our century, the gods of materialism, pleasure, sex and the occult all vie for the attention of unregenerate man. There is often a more conscious following after these things.

Man was made for relationship with a God who desires his worship. The pinnacle of Old Testament revelation came to Moses on Mount Sinai, when the ten commandments and the law of God were given. Amidst flashing lightning and peals of thunder, God revealed his righteous laws by which the human race was to live. The finger of God inscribed the words of the first commandment on one of the two stone tablets, challenging every man-made concept of God and every esoteric form of worship:

You shall have no other gods before Me. You shall not make for yourself an idol, or any likeness of what is in heaven above or on the earth beneath or in the water under the earth. You shall not worship them or serve them; for I, the Lord your God, am a jealous God, visiting the iniquity of the fathers on the children, on the third and fourth generations of those who hate Me, but showing lovingkindness to thousands, to those who love Me and keep My commandments (Ex 20:3-6).

God's special instructions to Israel set them apart as a nation through whom he would reveal himself to mankind. This revelation would culminate in the birth of the Messiah.

On the edge of entry into the promised land after forty years of wandering in the wilderness, Moses addressed the nation recalling all that God had said and done for them. Although the journey from Egypt to the promised land should have taken only eleven days, disobedience, grumbling and rebellion kept the children of Israel from their inheritance for forty years. Moses knew that God would not permit him to cross the Jordan; the time had come for his life and ministry to draw to a close. And so, in preparation for the entry into the promised land, Moses, the inspiration and leader of the people under God's direction, brought his final exhortations and warnings. The book of Deuteronomy records the words of Moses and focuses on the conditions of God's blessing in the promised land. If the people obeyed, God would bless; if they disobeyed and rebelled, various curses would follow. They were reminded of their uniqueness as a people and were warned to live a life of separation from the influences of other nations, their idolatry and its attendant practices.

Accompanying the promise of a land 'flowing with milk and honey' came the charge to obey the first commandment: 'Hear, O Israel! The Lord is our God, the Lord is one! And you shall love the Lord your God with all your heart and with all your soul and with all your might' (Deut 6:4). God was not expecting a slavish obedience to the rigours of an impossible law, but was looking for obedience flowing from a loving relationship. Love is at the heart of the law. Love for God was to be expressed in obedience. Idolatry would be unthinkable within a heart relationship with God, as would murder, covetousness, lying and adultery. The tragedy of Israel's inconsistencies and backslidings throughout her troubled history came about because her love for God regularly grew cold. Rebellion and idolatry were the inevitable results.

The old covenant provided God's law, but God's people could not keep it. God's master plan gradually unfolded as the prophets proclaimed a time when a new covenant would supercede the old. It would be a covenant based on a new relationship. The prophet Jeremiah looked down through the ages and prophesied about a new spiritual age:

> 'Behold, days are coming', declares the Lord, 'when I will make a new covenant with the house of Israel and with the house of Judah, not like the covenant which I made with their fathers in the day I took them by the hand to bring them out of the land of Egypt, My covenant, which they broke, although I was a husband to them,' declares the Lord. 'But this is the covenant which I will make with the house of Israel after those days,' declares the Lord, 'I will put My law within them, and on their heart I will write it; and I will be their God, and they shall be My people' (Jer 31:31-33).

The writer to the Hebrews, commenting on Jeremiah's prophecy, sheds light on the nature of this new covenant. In Hebrews chapter 9 he explains that the first covenant had rules and regulations which governed the practice of divine worship at the tabernacle. By an elaborate system of sacrifice, and with various representational objects such as a golden altar, a golden lampstand and the ark of the covenant, the priests performed their acts of worship on behalf of the people. The weakness of this form of worship was that it was unable to 'make the worshiper perfect in conscience' because the worship was related to outward form (Heb 9:9).

To obey God and love him from the heart would require a new covenant which would effect a change in the fundamental nature of man, giving him the ability to respond to God in a loving way. This new covenant would have to be mediated by someone able to reconcile a Holy God to a sinful human race. Jesus, God's Son, perfectly fulfilled every aspect of old covenant life, and so was able to mediate a new covenant. If God accepted the rituals of the old covenant as a means of sanctifying the flesh, 'how much more will the blood of Christ, who through the eternal Spirit offered Himself without blemish to God, cleanse your conscience from dead works to serve the living God?' (Heb 9:14).

Jesus' mission to the world was to make it possible for us to love God with our whole heart. His life and teaching, his death and resurrection, harmonized to effect a new covenant. The earthly life of Jesus testified to a loving relationship with his Father. His many confrontations with the legalistic Pharisees highlighted the stark contrast between the religious life conducted by rules and regulations, and the freedom and vibrancy of a heart relationship with God. During a time of interrogation by the Pharisees, a lawyer tested Jesus with a question:

> 'Teacher, which is the great commandment in the Law?' And He said to him, 'You shall love the Lord your God with all your heart, and with all your soul, and with all your mind.' This is the great and foremost commandment. And a second is like it, 'You shall love your neighbor as yourself.' On these two commandments depend the whole Law and the Prophets' (Mt 22:36-40).

Jesus' reply crystallized the nature and principle of new covenant life.

The nature of true worship

One day, Jesus was making the long journey from Judea to Galilee (Jn 4:3-29). The main route ran through Sychar, a Samaritan town. As Jesus, weary and travel-worn, approached the town he went to Jacob's well. The cool waters of the well would slake his aching thirst after the long and dusty road. A Samaritan woman approached to draw water. She was astonished and deeply curious when this Jewish man broke all the conventions by asking her, a Samaritan, and a woman at that, for water. Her amazement grew when he went on to talk about living water that she would need to draw from the well each day, and when he ended by telling her about her previous five husbands and that he knew that her current man wasn't her husband at all.

Understanding now that Jesus was a prophet, she began to engage him in conversation about worship. The Samaritans had conflicting ideas about worship from the Jews who regarded them as a schismatic race. They believed that Mount Gerizim and not Jerusalem was the place for sacrifice and worship. The discussion Jesus had with the Samaritan woman has much to teach us about true worship.

Not where, but how

'You worship that which you do not know' (Jn 4:22). Primarily, worship is for God. Therefore worship needs to be related to who God is, to his character and according to his workings. The more we know God, the more we will want to worship him.

A right understanding of the nature and character of God is essential for true worship. There must be freedom from man-made, intellectualized concepts of God, or we will be worshipping 'that which we do not know'. God has revealed himself through creation and our consciences, but the clearest revelation of all comes through the Bible and through the life of Jesus.

The Bible never argues for the existence of God. It is not a systematic theology or apologetic, but a supernaturally inspired collection of books through which God reveals his character and nature. God is described as loving, righteous, holy, patient, full of goodness, just, wrathful and yet merciful. The nature of God consists of a harmonizing blend of all his attributes. There are no inconsistencies or contradictions in his nature. Each attribute is an expression of the completeness of his being. He is all powerful, all knowing, and his presence pervades everything. His names represent different aspects of his character: *El Elym*—God most high; *El Olam*—the everlasting God; *El Shaddai*—God almighty; *Elohim* —God of creation and providence.

The most common name for God is 'Yahweh', often rendered 'Jehovah'. This name expresses God's self-existence and his eternal unchangeable character. There are also several covenant names: *Jehovah Jireh*—the Lord my provider; *Jehovah Nissi*—the Lord my banner; *Jehovah Tsidkenu*—the Lord my righteousness; *Jehovah Shalom*—the Lord my peace; *Jehovah Rophekah*—the Lord my healer. Throughout the Old Testament, as God deals with men and women in different situations, he is always seen to act consistently with his character. When we praise the name of the Lord, we should have in mind the comprehensiveness of his character expressed in his different names.

Jesus directed the Samaritan woman's attention on the fatherhood of God. He said that the true worshippers are those who worship the Father. To call God 'Father' implies a relationship. To worship God as Father implies a relationship of love. This is entered into through knowing Jesus and identifying with him. No one can come to the Father except through the Son. The Father's special relationship with Jesus becomes ours the moment we are in Christ. Paul, writing to the Philippians, explains that the true circumcision are those who 'worship in the Spirit of God and glory in Christ Jesus' (Phil 3:3).

It is not possible to worship God as Father without glorifying in Jesus the Son. The multitudes drawn from every tribe, tongue and nation, gathered around the throne in heaven, give glory to Jesus: 'Worthy is the Lamb that was slain to receive power and riches and wisdom and might and honour and glory and blessing' (Rev 5:12). Glory is given to Jesus because of the great work of salvation he has accomplished. Through his death on the cross we are reconciled to God. The new birth means that we are given a totally new nature by the Holy Spirit. God's laws are written on our hearts. The motivation to love and obey God replaces our rebellious, spiritually dead nature. The Christian life is not lived out by constantly trying to do the right thing. We do not achieve a right standing with God by our performance. The love of God has been 'poured out within our hearts through the Holy Spirit' (Rom 5:5). We respond to his Fatherhood. Our identity is in Jesus. We are radically different creatures with a new spiritual endowment. Loving God with all our heart, mind, soul and strength becomes our preoccupation. In so doing, we fulfil God's original intention—a harmonious relationship between God and his redeemed new creation.

Man's inbuilt desire and capacity for finding spiritual fulfilment and expressing worship, can only be satisfied by obedience to the first commandment. Through the death and resurrection of his Son, God has provided a way by which our rebellion towards him, and our tendency towards worshipping anything other than himself can be overcome. Joyful submission to a loving Father, expressed in worship and adoration, characterizes the true Christian as he lives out the new covenant life.

Jesus went on to tell the Samaritan woman that the true worshippers are those 'who worship . . . in the spirit and truth' (Jn 4:23). We worship the Father, Son and Holy Spirit. The Holy Spirit's ministry is to glorify Jesus and to testify to our sonship, giving us assurance of it as the Spirit within us cries, 'Abba, Father'.

The natural outflow of the Spirit-filled life is worship. When the apostles were baptized in the Holy Spirit on the Day of

Pentecost, they began speaking in tongues, magnifying and glorifying God. Speaking and singing in tongues releases the heart by the Holy Spirit to bring praise and worship to God in the dimension of the spirit. Where ordinary words fail, communing in tongues gives expression to our very deepest feelings about God. As we are filled with the Spirit, we can speak to one another in psalms, hymns and spiritual songs, singing and making melody with our hearts to the Lord (Eph 5:18-19).

We not only worship in the Spirit, but also in truth. We must beware an emphasis on subjectivity, experiences and feelings. God's truth remains constant and is an anchor when pressures, trials and circumstances would conspire to rob us of our joy. Faith in God's unchanging word will sustain us when we are battling with our emotions. By allowing the word to take root in our lives we will produce the fruit of worship: 'Let the word of Christ richly dwell within you, with all wisdom teaching and admonishing one another with psalms and hymns and spiritual songs, singing with thankfulness in your hearts to God' (Col 3:16).

Conclusion

True worship is not dependent on a particular situation or tradition, but is an expression of love and adoration to a loving heavenly Father. New covenant believers have the word and the Holy Spirit to enable them to bring to God the kind of worship he is seeking. The forms and traditions of worship in the old covenant have been superceded by the life and spirit of the new. Gatherings for worship in the early church gave opportunity for each member to participate with psalms, hymns and spiritual songs. The gifts of the Spirit were manifest, the word was preached and the body of believers was built up.

God is restoring true worship to his church by the creativity and vitality of the Spirit. God's purpose for the new covenant community is described in 1 Peter 2:9—'But you are a chosen race, a royal priesthood, a holy nation, a people for God's own possession, that you may proclaim the excellences of Him who called you out of darkness into His marvelous light.'

6

Expressions of Praise and Worship

Every Saturday afternoon from late August until early May, with colourful scarves, rattles, songs and chants, thousands of football supporters pay homage at various shrines to our national sport. Such displays of enthusiasm are rare in this laid-back, passive generation. Occasionally at royal weddings, general elections and cup finals, inhibitions are discarded in fervent demonstrations of loyalty. Balloons, streamers and banners add to the colour of such events. When it is all over there is always the armchair, the television and the video to restore our passivity to a bombardment of advertising tricks, trivial soap operas, and anything else the media can find to entertain a non-active, non-participating public.

Enthusiasm carries connotations of whole-hearted vigour. In most people's minds it has nothing remotely to do with God. That anyone could be enthusiastic about going to church, reading the Bible, praying or knowing God would come as a great surprise to them.

Like many words, enthusiasm has changed its meaning over the centuries. Originally it comes from the Greek *en theo* meaning 'inspired by' or 'possessed by' God. Just as the word 'Christian' was originally a derisive nickname for the believers in the early church, so in the eighteenth century the word 'enthusiast' became a derogative term for the early Methodists. The Holy Club in Oxford was a meeting place for John and Charles Wesley, George Whitefield and others. They had a zeal and fire which brought revival to Britain. When John Wesley described his experience of conversion as having 'his heart strangely warmed', it was in direct contrast to the barren othodoxy of the established church which regarded any zealous activity for God as dangerous. The labelling of these men as enthusiasts was meant to discredit them.

Jesus said that we are to love God with all our heart, mind, soul and strength. In other words, with every faculty of our personality and every ounce of our being. How extraordinary that so often church services lack the spark of life when the gospel gives us something to be really excited about. When John Bunyan described the conversion of Christian in *Pilgrim's Progress*, he clearly understood the joy that comes when there is forgiveness of sin:

> Then was Christian glad and lightsome, and said with a merry heart, He hath given me rest by His sorrows, and life by His death. Then he stood still awhile to look and wonder, for it was very surprising to him that the sight of the cross should thus ease him of his burden. He looked again even until the springs that were in his head sent waters down his cheeks. Then Christian gave three leaps for joy, and went on singing.

When Peter and John brought healing to the lame man at the Beautiful Gate he went on his way 'walking and leaping and praising God' (Acts 3:8). When a person has truly met with God they are filled with 'joy inexpressible and full of glory' (1 Pet 1:8). It is most unnatural to suppress the fruit of joy produced by the Holy Spirit, but do church services allow for devotion to God to be expressed demonstratively?

The Old Testament book of worship, the Psalms, conveys the whole range of human emotion in the way the songs give praise and worship to God. If these psalms were used to declare worship under the old covenant, how much more should they touch the imagination and quicken worship under the new. In the Psalms there are exhortations to sing, dance, shout, raise the hands, clap the hands, stand up, bow down and speak out. Worship which comes from the heart finds its expression through the actions of the body. True worship needs to be demonstrated.

In the new covenant our whole life declares worship to God as we present ourselves as living sacrifices to him. However, a further dimension is added to our worship when we participate with our whole heart, mind, soul and strength, engaging in bodily expressions as a means of communicating what is within us. Our mental, emotional, creative and physical capacities combine to give glory to God. The reality of our relationship with God, the fact that he lives within us, that we have experienced his love, and that we are in him, should produce unreserved expressions of love and devotion. Christians have a genuine *en theo* experience.

The ways in which worship can be expressed

1) Singing

Song is one of the simplest ways of communicating and releasing emotion. A contented baby readily responds to the gentle lullaby of a caring mother. The natural reaction of a child having received a birthday or Christmas gift is to sing and dance with joy. Whether it is the romance of a love song or the stirring patriotic strains of a national anthem, singing is an integral part of humanity. It is a gift to the human race from a God who himself loves to sing.

Joseph Gelineau comments on this gift:

> In singing, a man becomes as it were a pouring-out and a gift, because song, compounded of the breath which he breathes out from his inmost self and of the sound of his voice which cannot be held or imprisoned, is the free expression of himself, the manifestation of his interior being and the gratuitous giving of his personality. Brought face to face with entrancing beauty, man lifts up his heart in a cry of admiration; he comes forth from himself in the

sound of his voice, that he may be carried towards the object of his praise. Finally song is the living portrayal of spiritual self-giving. It is the gift of love whereby man sets himself free in a joyous abandonment and complete affirmation, knowing that precisely there, where he seems to lose himself is in fact where he finds and expresses himself to the full. His very being gushes forth under the impulse or attraction of love which his heart, overflowing or vanquished, is no longer able to contain.[7]

Although this is a rather idealized view of singing, it does reveal an intrinsic truth. Song is an effective means of self-expression. Singing can release what is in the very depths of the soul.

The most common Hebrew word for singing is *ranan*. It is used to convey great joy and exultation. It suggests loud exuberant singing. Other words for singing are *shur* and *zamar*, meaning to make music in praise of God'. Many different types of song are mentioned, particularly in the Psalms.

▶ Songs Praising God's name: Psalm 9:2—'I will sing praise to Thy name, O Most High.'

▶ Songs to the Lord: Psalm 13:6—'I will sing to the Lord, because He has dealt bountifully with me.'

▶ Songs of victory: Psalm 20:5—'We will sing for joy over your victory.' Songs of victory would have been heard after a battle had been won. The defeat of the Egyptians was celebrated with singing and dancing. Deborah's victory over the Canaanites was celebrated with a victory song, and in Revelation 15:3 the victorious company of the redeemed sing the song of Moses and of the Lamb. Songs extolling the victory of Christ over Satan should constantly be rising up in thankfulness to God.

▶ Songs declaring God's power: Psalm 21:13—'We will sing and praise Thy power.'

▶ Songs with instrumental accompaniment: Psalm 33:2—

'Give thanks to the Lord with the lyre; sing praises to Him with a harp of ten strings.'

▶ New songs: Psalm 33:3—'Sing to Him a new song.'

▶ Songs focusing on God's sovereignty: Psalm 47:6—'Sing praises to our King.'

▶ Songs expressing skill and creativity: Psalm 47:6—'Sing praises with a skilful psalm'

▶ Songs about God's righteousness: Psalm 51:14—'My tongue will joyfully sing of Thy righteousness.' Psalm 51 is a song of repentance. David is seeking forgiveness and restoration after his sin of adultery and murder, and is longing to be able to sing with a clean heart of the righteousness of God.

▶ Songs declaring God's prophetic purpose: Psalm 67:4—'Let the nations be glad and sing for joy; for Thou wilt judge the peoples with uprightness, and guide the nations on the earth. Let the peoples praise Thee, O God; Let all the peoples praise Thee. The earth has yielded its produce; God, our God, blesses us. God blesses us, that all the ends of the earth may fear Him.'

▶ Songs about God's character: Psalm 89:1—'I will sing of the loving kindness of the Lord forever.'

▶ Songs about God's actions: Psalm 92:4—'I will sing for joy at the works of Thy hands.'

▶ Songs about God's word: Psalm 119:172—'Let my tongue sing of Thy word.'

▶ Songs of thanksgiving: Psalm 147:7—'Sing to the Lord with thanksgiving.'

▶ Songs of deliverance: Psalm 32:7—'Thou dost surround me with songs of deliverance.' Could it be that in times of distress or trial God actually sings songs of deliverance for our protection and comfort? Perhaps this could refer to us taking encouragement from what is being sung by those around us in the church? In either case, it is possible to experience deliverance through the ministry of singing.

▶ Songs in the night: Job 35:10—'God my Maker, who gives songs in the night.'

Singing is not just for when we are feeling exuberant and joyful. It can also help in times of sadness and difficulty. A young married couple in my church, Brian and Claire, is the kind every pastor enjoys having in his congregation. They run the mid-week children's club, are keen evangelists, and real participants in our times of worship. When Claire became pregnant, their excitement could hardly be contained. Within two days of the birth of a beautiful daughter, Brian was summoned to the hospital and informed that the baby had a serious heart defect. Within hours the baby had died, and when I visited them in the hospital ward we wept together, too stunned even to speak.

They came to stay with my wife, Rosie, and myself for a few days, when we sought to help them in their recovery. Even though their hearts were grieving and their questions taxed any kind of understanding of God's working, they were still able to sing of the faithfulness and love of God as they walked through the valley of the shadow of death. Their songs in the night helped them express their grief, but also strengthened them to continue in their faith.

These different types of song not only cover all aspects of God's character and ways, but also provide a means of expressing ourselves to God. There is much scope for creativity without slipping into sentimentality. In recent years many new songs have been inspired by the Holy Spirit, and there are many resources available for churches to keep a freshness in the songs they sing. A good Christian song should contain sound doctrine with melodies appropriate for corporate singing. Words of Scripture are particularly helpful. Many great hymns of the past complement these new songs. Such hymns as 'The God of Abraham praise', 'A debtor to mercy alone' and 'Join all the glorious names' contain great doctrinal statements of faith. And there are many more.

Congregational singing gives corporate expression to an identifiable truth. Faith comes by hearing the word of God, and when a congregation in Spirit-led worship sings the truth of God's word, we can expect a growth in faith among those who are singing. It is the word not the song that engenders faith, but when the singing carries the word with it faith can be increased. This happened in a gathering I can recall where the song 'Blessed be the God and Father of our Lord Jesus Christ' was being repeatedly sung with a real sense of God's anointing. Many testified to receiving revelation of the Fatherhood of God and of their security in his never-failing love. The word of God brought revelation, inspired faith, and changed people's lives.

Singing can also bring a sense of God's presence. God is omnipresent, he is always with us, but there are times when he loves to manifest himself. He is enthroned on the praises of his people, and when a company of worshippers together bring their praises, love and adoration, God delights to come in glory and power. When Solomon had completed the Temple, the priests came to minister to the Lord in praise and worship. The glory of God came down, and they were unable to stand up in the presence of God.

Psalm 68:4 says, 'Sing to God, sing praises to His name; cast up a highway for Him who rides through the deserts, whose name is the Lord, and exult before Him.' However, we must beware of simply using singing to create an artificial atmosphere which we mistake as the presence of God, or to try to manipulate the Holy Spirit into manifesting himself. God is seeking true worshippers and true songs of praise rising from the inspiration of the Spirit and the truth of God's word. This is the only way by which a highway may be cast up for God. The one who delights in the praises of his people will come down that highway, manifesting his presence in the midst of a truly worshipping company.

That God responds to praise is illustrated by the events recorded in Acts 16 when Paul and Silas went to Philippi. Having created a commotion in the city by their preaching, they were beaten up, thrown into prison and securely fastened in the stocks. At midnight Paul and Silas, instead of giving in to the pain and difficulty of their situation, sang hymns of praise to God. The other prisoners must have marvelled at how anybody in their plight could have even had the strength to sing, let alone the motivation.

Suddenly the praise session was interrupted by an earthquake which opened all the prison doors and loosened the fetters binding the prisoners. As a result, the jailer was converted and Paul and Silas were able to go free. There is no suggestion that the two apostles were praising to create an effect, or that they even expected such a powerful manifestation of God's presence. Their songs in the night were the outflow of love and thanksgiving. It was natural for them to praise God, and he was certainly enthroned on their praises that particular night.

Singing releases the heart, expresses emotion, helps us meditate on truth, and provides a means for a congregation to declare the truth together.

2) Singing in the spirit

Singing in the spirit (or, more accurately, singing by the spirit) is a way by which we can express our innermost heart to God. When we speak in tongues we speak mysteries. When these mysteries are combined with melodies, there may be a release of love and adoration that goes beyond speech.

In Revelation chapter 1 the voice of Jesus is described as 'like the sound of many waters'. In chapter 14 John recounts his vision of the Lamb of God standing on Mount Zion with the whole company of the redeemed. He describes an incredible aural phenomenon:

> And I heard a voice from heaven, like the sound of many waters
> and like the sound of loud thunder, and the voice which I heard
> was like the sound of harpists playing on their harps. Any they

sang a new song before the throne and before the four living creatures and the elders; and no one could learn the song except the one hundred and forty-four thousand who had been purchased from the earth.

This is reminiscent of the sound of a large number of people singing in tongues all together. When a whole congregation lifts up its voice as one in a harmonic blend of sound, singing a new song which nobody else can learn or understand, the resonance and tenor are evocative of a cascading waterfall. Could this be 'the sound of many waters' that John heard? It is possible that the voice of Jesus, rejoicing in song in the midst of the children he has been given by his Father (Heb 2:12-13) has an aural realization when the body of Jesus joins in that song as it is inspired by the Spirit?

When a voice came from the throne saying, 'Give praise to our God, all you His bond-servants, you who fear Him, the small and the great' (Rev 19:5), the response to the voice was the sound of many waters arising from a great multitude, combined with the sound of mighty peals of thunder, saying, 'Hallelujah! For the Lord our God, the Almighty, reigns. Let us rejoice and be glad and give glory to Him' (Rev 19:6-7). The congregation before the throne sings a new song. It is like the sound of many waters. It is supplemented with expressions of vocal praise with intelligible content. What John heard in the spirit probably had a reference point on earth, or his readers would not have understood what he was writing about.

Although corporate singing in the spirit is not explicitly referred to in Scripture, the worship in the book of Revelation implies that it could have existed in the early church. When the voice of the congregation is lifted up in one accord, singing under the inspiration of the Holy Spirit, worship is lifted into an eternal heavenly realm and God draws very near. Songs extolling God's character, songs in praise of Jesus, interjected with spontaneous singing in the spirit, shouts of joyful acclamation, and hushed bowing in the presence of God, are all features of Spirit-inspired worship. The result is a glorious symphonic paean of praise, composed not by any musical genius but by the creative Spirit of God breathing life into a willing and available church.

3) Prophetic singing

At David's Tabernacle there seems to have been what could be described as a prophetic singing workshop. 1 Chronicles 25 describes how the musicians and singers would come together under King David's direction to prophesy in song and with their instruments. Asaph, Heman and Jeduthun directed their families in prophesying, in giving thanks, and praising the Lord. Singers and instrumentalists were appointed and trained to give a musical lead to the congregation of Israel.

In the context of a church meeting (1 Cor 14:26), there is no reason why prophecies should not be sung as well as spoken. A prophetic exhortation or admonition in song can be very effective. Music helps to communicate words, and when the music and the content of the words are Spirit-inspired, there can be a much greater openness to what God is saying. I have often experienced meetings where there has been a time of singing in the spirit, followed by a prophetic song. On one particular occasion the congregation was singing, 'Father we love You, we worship and adore You, glorify Your name in all the earth.' Following the song there was a time of corporate singing in the spirit during which a prophetic song came forth about God's glory. The content of the prophetic song contained elements of exhortation and admonition as it focussed on being merciful, compassionate and kind so that God's glory would be revealed in us by our character as we lived in obedience to God. The sung prophecy was further underlined in the preaching which followed.

To allow for prophetic singing is to fulfil the promise of restoring David's Tabernacle. Prophetic singing provides opportunities to exhort, encourage and admonish by psalms, hymns and spiritual songs.

4) Antiphonal singing

A feature of some psalm singing was the dividing of the congregation into two groups, with each group singing a line or a phrase in turn. It is possible that Psalm 136 was sung in this way. Group 1 would sing, 'Give thanks to the Lord, for He is good,' while group 2 would respond, 'For His loving-kindness is everlasting.'

When Nehemiah completed the rebuilding of the walls of Jerusalem, Davidic worship was also restored. Two choirs were established to lead the praise, and the sound was so great that 'the joy of Jerusalem was heard from afar' (Neh 12:43). In re-establishing worship in Jerusalem according to the command of David, these antiphonal choirs would have given a lead to the congregation.

5) Responsive singing

Some psalms, such as Psalm 98, require a response from the congregation. It is possible that one of the masters of the singing, Chenaniah or Asaph, would have declared, 'O sing to the Lord a new song. . . .' The congregation would then respond, 'Shout joyfully to the Lord, all the earth.' These exhortations would be meaningless unless they met with the appropriate response. The exhortation, 'Sing praises to the Lord with the lyre,' would be met by the singers and lyre players. The orchestral tone colour would increase to the exhortation 'With trumpets and the sound of the horn.' 'Shout joyfully before the King, the Lord,' would elicit a further response from the congregation. The psalm, instead of being a poem to be read, becomes a means of expressing praise. As the master of singing pronounces his exhortations, so the orchestra and congregation respond.

6) Raising the hands

Raising the hands is a very simple means of showing love to God. A small child stretches his hands up to a parent for a loving cuddle or to attract attention. There is a simplicity and a deep trust in this action. When we raise our hands in worship it helps us to release any inhibitions. How wonderful to have such a close relationship with our loving Father that we can raise our hands in simple dependence and trust without condemnation and fear. When Cain sinned his 'countenance fell', he could not look up. When we know forgiveness we can look up, with hands raised, knowing that we are accepted and loved.

We raise our hands to:

▶ Bless the Lord—'Lift up your hands to the sanctuary, and bless the Lord' (Ps 134:2).

▶ Dedicate Ourselves—'May my prayer be counted as incense before Thee; the lifting up of my hands as the evening offering' (Ps 141:2).

▶ Express Desire—'I stretch out my hands to Thee; my soul longs for Thee, as a parched land' (Ps 143:6).

▶ Intercede—'Therefore I want the men in every place to pray, lifting up holy hands, without wrath and dissension' (1 Tim 2:8).

7) Clapping hands

The injunction to clap the hands in Scripture is to do with lauding (applauding) the King. At a coronation the new monarch would be acclaimed with shouts and applause. Clapping can also be a sign of rejoicing. (Scripture does not connect it with clapping to the beat in music or chorus singing.) Psalm 47:1 exhorts, 'O clap hands, all peoples; shout to God with the voice of joy,' and Psalm 98:8 declares, 'Let the rivers clap their hands; let the mountains sing together for joy.'

8) Dance

Just as song is a means of self-expression, so is dance. Dance is more controversial in worship because of its immediate visual impact and the danger of sensuality. Like all the creative gifts, dance in and of itself is neither moral nor immoral. It is how man uses movement and what he communicates through it that brings dance into the moral realm.

God himself created dance, and he loves to participate in it. Zephaniah describes how God feels about his people, 'The Lord your God is in your midst, a victorious warrior. He will exult over you with joy, He will be quiet in His love, He will rejoice over you with shouts of joy' (Zeph 3:17). The Hebrew word used here for rejoice is *gil*, which means to spin around in delirious delight as a result of great emotion.

If God is in the midst of his people, rejoicing over them with dancing, why should his people not join in and dance with him? Miriam rejoiced with dancing over the defeat of the Egyptians; David danced with all his might before the Lord; and Psalm 150:4 says, 'Praise Him with timbrel and dancing.' When Jeremiah prophesied a time of restoration after the Babylonian captivity, he described it as a time of great rejoicing: 'Again I will build you, and you shall be rebuilt, O virgin of Israel! Again you shall take up your tambourines, and go forth to the dances of the merrymakers' (Jer 31:4) 'Then the virgin shall rejoice in the dance, and the young men and the old, together' (Jer 31:13). The Hebrew word for dance here is *mecholah*, which means a communal or round dance.

▶ Dance as an expression of community.

In many folk cultures dancing in community, with older and younger generations participating, is an integral part of the people's heritage. This would have been the case with the Hebrews. Why shouldn't this be true in the kingdom of God, with dance as an expression of kingdom community life? It is part of our biblical heritage. Simple steps to current songs can easily be devised, with parents and children joining in during the worship time.

▶ Dance as an expression of joy.

The most common form of dance in the church today is a jigging up and down from one foot to the other.

This requires very little skill and some have labelled it the 'charismatic hop'. True joy does need to give vent to physical expression. The walking and leaping of the lame man healed at the gate of the Temple was a spontaneous action. He didn't worry about whether the religious authorities in the Temple approved. God had met him so he leaped for joy.

▶ Dance as an expression of truth.

We are living in a visual age. People respond more readily to visual communication than verbal. Creative dance can be very helpful in interpreting truth. Just as music enhances words, so can movement. Providing there are safeguards against sensuality, a solo dancer or group of dancers under the anointing of the creative Spirit of God can minister pure worship to God that is in Spirit and in truth.

The week after Keith Green was so tragically killed in a plane crash, I attended a meeting where a Christian professional dancer danced an interpretation of his setting of Psalm 23. It was both moving and reassuring as the confidence of fearing no evil in the valley of the shadow of death was interpreted through movement. Movement in dance is closely linked to that of drama. On several occasions in the Scriptures, dramatic mime is used to convey truth. Jeremiah smashed an earthenware vessel. Mary anointed Jesus' feet with her tears and with precious ointment and then wiped it away with her hair. The prophet Agabus acted out a prophecy of what was about to happen to Paul when he took Paul's belt and bound his own hands and feet with it.

Dance expressing personal joy and community life and dance interpreting the truth can enhance worship.

9) Bowing

The first commandment forbids bowing down to, or worshipping, any false god. To bow down implies submitting to, reverencing and worshipping something. A day is coming when the whole creation must submit to God and bow down to him. 'All mankind will come to bow down before Me,' says the Lord (Is 66:23). 'Therefore also God highly exalted Him, and bestowed on Him the name which is above every name, that at the name of Jesus every knee should bow' (Phil 2:9-10)

The physical act of bowing or kneeling or lying prostrate, arising out of submissive, adoring hearts, is a way of giving God worship. It also speaks of that day when 'every knee [shall] bow'. Those who love God are not coerced into this action. It is a voluntary movement in response to grace.

10) Shouting

A time of worship should be a time of rich variety. There is a time to be silent and a time to shout. Just as silence need not be deadly or awkward, so shouting does not have to be an empty noise. The worship John described in Revelation has times of thunderous sound as well as times of awed silence. There are times when it is right to shout acclamations to the King: 'Shout joyfully to the Lord, all the earth. Serve the Lord with gladness; come before Him with joyful singing' (Ps 100:1-2) Praise and worship from the heart needs to find full expression through the body. Man is a complete being, and the worship that God desires involves all aspects of the personality: spirit, mind, will, emotions and body.

When a congregation gathers to worship there can be corporate singing, singing in the spirit, prophetic song, antiphonal singing, and responsive singing combined with hand raising, times of joyful shouting, bowing and kneeling, silence, dance and movement, and spoken declarations of praise. There is no room for passivity. Each member of the congregation may participate in the flow of the Spirit at any particular moment. A time of worship should not be a spectator activity.

A worship meeting, however, is not a free-for-all. There needs to be both freedom and form. We need to understand the role of the church leaders, the worship leader, the musicians and the congregation if a church is going to be a worshipping community based on God's revelation in his word regarding how we worship. More of this in the next chapter.

7

The Worshipping Church

So be it, Lord! Thy throne shall never,
Like earth's proud empires, pass away;
Thy kingdom stands, and stands for ever,
Till all Thy creatures own Thy sway.

These words held a real poignancy as we concluded John
Ellerton's great hymn. I was sitting in a pew engraved with the
name of Castlereagh, the great British statesman of the
nineteenth century. The chancel of the Royal Chapel in
Windsor Castle is a fascinating place. The sense of history, the
colourful banners and the splendid architecture all combine to
speak of a remarkable heritage. I had never felt so British. I
ruminated on a lost empire, and as the vocal purity of the
chapel choir re-echoed the final strains of the hymn, I was full
of gratitude that the ephemeral empires of earth cannot com-
pare with the eternal stability of the kingdom of God. I love
my country and its heritage, but that love can never match the
love and commitment to a kingdom that cannot be shaken.

The service which I was attending was rich in tradition,
ritual and aesthetic pleasure. I had just played the trumpet in
St George's, Windsor, and had a general sense of well being.

The tragedy is that many people would regard the dignity, the tradition and the aesthetic qualities of the organ and choir as a religious experience. I found the experience artistically pleasing, but wondered what it had to do with worship in spirit and in truth.

It was a far cry from the throbbing bass drum and bass guitar, the handclapping, the leaping and shouting singers, the funky riffs on the brass and the gyrations around the stage of the Hammersmith Odeon as Andrae Crouch and the Disciples led the packed audience through 'Hallelujah', 'Revive us again', and 'Power in the blood'. The combination of jazz-funk, black gospel and extreme pentecostalism left the audience in frenzied excitement. I was as stirred by this as I was moved by the beauty of the Royal Chapel. However, I could not say with integrity that either experience was a genuine expression of worship in spirit and in truth.

It is possible to move from church to church until you find a style of worship that fits in with your cultural views and temperament. True worship, however, is nothing to do with temperament. With so much revelation in Scripture as to how we should worship, it is important that values, opinions and judgements are formed in the light of God's word. The way we worship should not be dictated by culture or tradition. Even allowing for a wide diversity within the body of Christ, there are certain principles which need to be observed. To understand how a church should worship there needs to be an understanding of the doctrine of the church.

A church consists of a redeemed company of people. For a church to enter into corporate dimensions of worship, it must consist of worshippers. The concept of a church with a mixture of saved and unsaved, wheat and tares, is unbiblical. The church is God's redeemed community. The people in the church are worshippers because they love God. That is not to say that the unsaved cannot attend. In a truly worshipping church, where the presence of God is manifested, it is good for the unsaved to attend. They are very likely to encounter God as he is being worshipped by his people. The attendance of the unsaved can provide an excellent evangelistic opportunity. But it is not until people are themselves Christians that they become part of the church. The opinions about worship expressed by unsaved visitors will have, at best, little relevance.

A worshipping church is made up of people who each have a relationship with God and who love him individually. When they come together, all the dimensions of worship already discussed should be evident. During a period of time in a gathered committed church, the worship should include corporate singing, singing in the spirit, instrumental accompaniment, dance, shouting, applauding, quietness, stillness, spontaneous outbursts of joy, all expressing outwardly our inward response to our salvation. Within the congregational gathering there should be opportunities for teaching, exhortations and the exercise of spiritual gifts as well as the all important preaching of the word. Worship gatherings should not be so aesthetically contrived that spontaneity is crushed; neither should they be free for alls under the guise of the 'freedom of the Spirit'.

Leadership

If a church is going to develop in worship, there needs to be a clear understanding of leadership in the local church. Problems abound when a pastor does not have the same vision for charismatic life as his church members. Pressure groups can create tensions and relationship difficulties, often hiving off into a mid-week charismatic group meeting in secret for fear that under the pastor their church will not achieve the kind of worship God desires. On the other hand, the envisioned pastor will not inspire confidence in his flock if one Sunday the conventional hymnal is being used as it always has been, and the next Sunday the pews have disappeared along with the hymn books and the organ. Without being prepared by careful teaching and sensitive envisioning, people will not take readily to overhead projectors, the latest worship songs, hand-raising and dancing. Such changes need informed minds, softened spirits and warmed hearts.

Leaders need to be sensitive to their people, while people need to be submissive to their leaders. Living worship should be an expression of the whole church. True, individuals bring their own love to God, but a church is made up of a company of worshippers. Any attempt to introduce living worship into an unyielding situation because of either leadership prejudice or congregational prejudice will not work.

What happens on a Sunday morning in the worship service should be a reflection of what is happening in terms of fellowship and community life during the week. Worship is integral to the whole life of the church. Thus the responsibility of church leadership is to encourage a church to become a worshipping church.

Leadership and worship as a priority

Regular teaching needs to be given to help people become true worshippers. The preaching of the great doctrines of the Christian faith will draw people closer to God, but they also need to develop the ability to apply these doctrines. To have a right doctrine of the Trinity is vital; to understand the work of the Holy Spirit is essential; but if our understanding is purely cerebral, our worship will be cold and formal. We best understand the Holy Spirit by being completely available to him.

Preaching the baptism in the Holy Spirit and then leading people into the experience will have a significant impact on the worship. Preaching the grace of God and getting people to understand their position in Christ will result in an abundant outpouring of gratitude and worship.

In the first chapter of his letter to the Ephesians, Paul states the doctrines relating to our salvation: 'He chose us in Him before the foundation of the world'; 'He predestined us to adoption as sons'; 'In him we have redemption through His blood; the forgiveness of our trespasses, according to the riches of his grace which he lavished upon us'; 'You were sealed in Him with the Holy Spirit of promise.' The result of this great salvation is that we live 'to the praise of His glory'. To know that God has called us and chosen us, even before we were born, and that we are predestined to be conformed to the image of his son; that we are justified freely by grace and that there is no condemnation in Christ; that God is absolutely committed to us and that we are eternally secure in his unfailing love, must surely result in joyful, exuberant thanksgiving and praise.

Leaders not only need to preach about worship, or the doctrines that lead to people becoming worshippers; they also need to encourage participation; and structure the gatherings accordingly. At first a few brave people may begin to raise their hands during the singing of the last verse of the hymn. Then, as new songs are taught, people may start clapping to the rhythm of the song. Certain songs lend themselves to some form of response. 'I lift up my hands in Your name' cannot be sung with integrity without the action being performed. As boldness increases, dancing in the aisles and even some singing in the spirit may find their way into the meeting.

The organist of a church which I once attended became increasingly alarmed at the desire of the congregation to sing Scripture choruses. 'Sheer cant!' was his indignant comment as he saw his church come alive in the Spirit. To those trained in the ways of the Royal School of Church Music, the culture shock of such expressions of worship may be just too much to bear. Love and sensitivity are essential in leading a church on in God's purpose. So, too, is a real understanding of the teaching of Scripture that may well lead to radical change.

Leadership and worship leaders

There are times when a church leader or leadership team may want to encourage the development of worship, but they lack musical skill and feel intimidated by the thought of leading charismatic worship. It is important to develop the ministry of others in this particular area. Find a competent worship leader and sympathetic musicians to help give a lead. Develop a team of instrumentalists and singers to hold worship workshops. The relationship between church leaders and musicians is vital if a church is going to be effective in worship.

Prophetic vision

The renewal of worship is not something to brighten up church services. In a recent national poll on church attendance, a large percentage of the people interviewed said that they thought the church was outdated because of outmoded, irrelevant forms of worship. The contemporary worship scene, with its middle-of-the-road type popular music, has a broad appeal. The danger is that the musical style and outward form can be an end in itself. Renewed worship is not ultimately to make Christianity more relevant to our culture, though this may be a result. Renewed worship is an integral part of what God is doing today in bringing the church back to how God intended it to be: worship is an essential part of God's restoration programme.

We have already observed that the Apostle James saw the church as the prophetic fulfilment of the words of Amos regarding the restoration of David's Tabernacle. This being so, there are radical implications not only for our worship but also for our vision. Many of the Psalms (e.g. Psalms 2 and 10) point to the establishing of God's kingdom throughout the earth. Jesus' coming totally fulfilled these prophetic scriptures, but there is a sense in which they are continually being fulfilled as the church, the body of Christ, is being restored. The purpose of the church's restoration is 'that the rest of mankind may seek the Lord' (Acts 15:17).

God is not restoring the church just to produce better or more living worship. There is a definite evangelistic implication of bringing the gospel of the kingdom to the nations. When the Holy Spirit initially moves upon a church, the raising of hands or dancing may seem a bold expression of release from the empty forms and stale traditions of much evangelicalism. But God has a bigger purpose than getting us to 'stick 'em up!' Jesus came for the world; he wants a church throughout the ends of the earth:

> As a result of the anguish of His soul, He will see it and be satisfied (Is 53:11),
> For Zion's sake I will not keep silent, and for Jerusalem's sake I will not keep quiet, until her righteousness goes forth like brightness, and her salvation like a torch that is burning. And the nations will see your righteousness, and all kings your glory; and you will be called by a new name, which the mouth of the Lord will designate. You will also be a crown of beauty in the hand of the Lord, and a royal diadem in the hand of your God (Is 62:1-3).

If a church begins to worship according to biblical principles, with vitality, spontaneity, every member functioning and each one having a contribution, then every aspect of its life will be challenged. Many issues will need to be addressed, from theological questions about baptism in the Holy Spirit and church leadership, to the more mundane problems of seating arrangements and projectors. A church that wants to fulfil God's purpose in being a worshipping community will need to examine carefully every aspect of its life and belief in the light of God's word. For this reason the initial move of the Holy Spirit in the early 60s led many to look beyond the personal implications of baptism in the Spirit and renewed worship to reconsider the kind of church that was really on God's heart. God was not only renewing but was also seeking to restore and recover a lost church.

As he has gone about his restoring work, the Holy Spirit has brought different emphases at various times and these emphases were often reflected in songs. Truths about our fellowship together, declarations of faith, expressions of worship and insights about the kingdom were re-examined through the many new worship songs which began to appear. As these songs became popular, people found themselves singing truths that affected their church life. It is not possible for a church to sing Graham Kendrick's song 'Jesus stand among us' without fellowship being enhanced and prophetic vision being clarified. Today there are many new songs which express God's prophetic word to his church. To sing these songs without being in the reality of the truth they proclaim is hypocrisy.

With the development of worship through the 60s and 70s and with the growing vision of restoration, came a greater understanding of spiritual authority, Ephesians 4 ministries, personal commitment to the body, and a greater understanding of the grace of God. (For a fuller understanding of the principles of restoration, read *Restoration in the Church* by Terry Virgo (Kingsway 1985).)

A worshipping church, then, is a church whose worship is in spirit and in truth, making room for a whole range of expressions. A theology which embraces the implications of biblical worship will inevitably have to face issues like the grace of God, prophetic vision, apostolic and prophetic ministry, plurality of leadership, spiritual authority and submission, evangelism, and each member of the church functioning. There also needs to be a flexibility in church life and structure to allow for this living worship to happen. The lay-out of seating, use of overhead projectors, sensitive musicians, and an envisioned leadership will all help to make theology a reality.

8

Gathering for Worship

'You don't have to go to church to be a Christian' is a comment often made by people who seek to excuse themselves from any responsibility towards God. It represents a misunderstanding of what the church is. Victor Hugo said that the church was God between four walls, again missing the essential nature of the church.

Our word 'church' is an Anglo-Saxon translation of the Greek word *ecclesia* which means 'to be called out for a purpose'. In Greece an ecclesia would be called if there was a political statement to be made or to impart news. The church is a people who have been called out and gathered for a purpose. That purpose is primarily to worship God. Christians don't go to church; they are the church. The gathering of themselves together gives them visibility and identity.

The concept of gathering is deeply rooted in Old Testament life. The congregation was assembled by Moses at the time of the Passover, and during the forty years of wandering through the wilderness there would have been special times when the people congregated. The focal point of these gatherings was the Tabernacle. During the period of David's reign, too, there would be times of gathering to worship at the Tabernacle, and the Psalms make reference to the great congregation. There were also times of special festival gatherings like the Feast of Tabernacles. The emphasis of the feasts of Israel was on celebrating what God had done for them and joyfully looking forwards to future blessings.

In New Testament times the church gathered together on a regular basis. Right from the outset in Acts 2 we see the early church gathering together in an area of the Temple known as Solomon's Portico. This stretched along the east side of the Temple for 480 metres and was over 40 metres wide in its narrowest place. This huge area was the place where thousands of believers gathered in the early days of the church in Jerusalem. They also gathered in smaller groups in one another's homes.

In both the Old Testament and the New, the purpose of the people of God gathering together was to meet with God. As they assembled at the Tabernacle, the glory of God would fill that place and they knew that God was with them. When the early church gathered, God's presence was manifested among them. Even a superficial reading of Acts shows the power of God in the midst of the gathered church. There was a sense of awe as people were saved, and there were signs and wonders. People were either totally committed to this community or they dared not join because the fear of God was so great.

Outlined in Hebrews chapter 10 are some important principles governing the gathering of a congregation. The contrast between the old and new covenants is drawn, although there are lessons to be learned from the old:

> Since therefore, brethren, we have confidence to enter the holy place by the blood of Jesus, by a new and living way which He inaugurated for us through the veil, that is, His flesh, and since we have a great priest over the house of God, let us draw near with a sincere heart in full assurance of faith, having our hearts sprinkled clean from an evil conscience and our bodies washed with pure water. Let us hold fast the confession of our hope without wavering, for He who promised is faithful; and let us consider how to stimulate one another to love and good deeds, not forsaking our

own assembling together, as is the habit of some, but encouraging
one another; and all the more, as you see the day drawing near
(Heb 10:19-25).

Under the old covenant, God's dwelling was the
Tabernacle or the Temple. The people went to the house of
God. There was an elaborate system of sacrifice, blood being
shed in order that God could be approached. There was a
priesthood who mediated between the people and God. However, their experience of God was real and the people did
participate. They would enter the gates of the Tabernacle
with thanksgiving and enter into the courts with praise (Ps
100:4). Even under the old covenant, God was seeking people
who worshipped from the heart and not just with a knowledge
of the correct ritual: 'Burnt offering and sin offering Thou
hast not required'. Then I said, 'Behold, I come; in the scroll
of the book it is written of me; I delight to do Thy will, O my
God; Thy Law is within my heart' (Ps 40:6-8).

Under the new covenant, God's dwelling is his people. We
are his temple. Individually our bodies are the temple of the
Holy Spirit, but there is also a sense in which together we are
being built into this temple: 'The whole building, being fitted
together is growing into a holy temple in the Lord; in whom
you also are being built together into a dwelling of God in the
Spirit' (Eph 2:21-22).

The Greek word used here for temple is *naos* which is the
word used in the Septuagint for the Holy of Holies, the place
where God's glory was revealed. God's dwelling-place is the
church. We don't go to the house of God; we are the house of
God. The sacrifice has been made once and for all, and we have
confidence before God by the blood of Jesus. We no longer
need a mediating priesthood; we are a royal priesthood.

Our assembling together, therefore, is an integral part of
our spiritual life. Together we are the temple of God, and it is
still God's heart to manifest himself, bringing glory to the
temple. When God's people gather, then, they should expect
to meet with God. Just as the old covenant worshippers

entered the Temple with thanksgiving and praise, so too as we gather for worship, there should be thanksgiving and praise on our lips as we approach God through that new and living way, the blood of Jesus.

When the walls of Jerusalem had been completed through the ministry of Nehemiah, and after the joyful celebrations with the singers and musicians, complacency and apathy began to creep in. The Levites and singers who performed the service had gone away, each to his own field. Nehemiah had to stir them and encourage them to fulfil their ministry of praise and worship. We must not neglect our assembling together, for when we gather we can expect to meet with God.

To love the church means to love the place where God lives. When I was a child I used to love visiting my grand-mother's house, not because of the journey, not because of the house itself, not even because of treats I could expect. I loved to visit my grandmother's house because my grand-mother was there. It is the same with the church: 'How lovely are Thy dwelling places, O Lord of hosts! My soul longed and even yearned for the courts of the Lord' (Ps 84:1). 'I was glad when they said to me, "Let us go to the house of the Lord"' (Ps 122:1) The gathering of God's people as they congregate together should be an event.

▶ A place of thanksgiving and praise: 'I will give Thee thanks in the great congregation; I will praise Thee among a mighty throng' (Ps 35:18).

▶ A place of proclamation: 'I have proclaimed glad tidings of righteousness in the great congregation' (Ps 40:9).

▶ A place where God's presence is experienced: 'God takes His stand in His own congregation' (Ps 82:1).

▶ A place of singing: 'Sing to the Lord a new song, and His praise in the congregation of the godly ones' (Ps 149:1).

▶ A place of released worship: In the congregation 'Let Israel be glad in his Maker; let the sons of Zion rejoice in their King. Let them praise His name with dancing; let them sing praises to Him with timbrel and lyre' (Ps 149:2-3).

▶ A place of mutual fellowship and encouragement: 'Let us consider how to stimulate one another to love and good deeds, not forsaking our own assembling together . . . but encouraging one another' (Heb 10:24-25).

▶ A place for the exercise of gifts and ministries: 'When you assemble, each one has a psalm, has a teaching, has a revelation, has a tongue, has an interpretation. Let all things be done for edification' (1 Cor 14:26).

Gatherings of the church should pulsate with the vigorous energy of a God who loves to be present with his people. There should be a total absence of passivity as God's people participate in the dynamics of congregational life.

Three levels of gathering

In the Old Testament the gatherings of the congregation had a celebratory aspect. Although there was participation, the praise and the music were led by musical priests who were chosen and appointed to their task (see chapter 4). In New Testament gatherings there is the same emphasis on participation, but there appears to be more room for individual contribution. The participation in the Old Testament appears largely to have been corporate. Singing, shouting, applauding, proclaiming and dancing appear to have been led by the musicians while the congregation would have participated corporately. In the New Testament meeting, 'each one' has a contribution. As the New Testament meetings would have taken the synagogue for their model, their size and format would have allowed for the type of meeting described in 1 Corinthians 14:26. There were also meetings in homes for the breaking of bread and for fellowship.

It would appear that there are three levels of gathering in

the Scriptures (see chapter 2): the large celebratory festival type gathering; the smaller congregational gathering where individuals can participate; and small 'cell' gatherings in homes for fellowship. Today many growing churches are finding the need to include these different types of meeting in their corporate life.

In the early years of Clarendon church, our life together consisted of two levels of meeting: the congregation and the cell. Occasionally we would gather with other churches and have a celebration, and we would annually attend the Downs Bible Week where thousands would gather for a time of celebration and festival. Our congregational meetings had a strong emphasis on each member participating, in the context of a worship time which included all the elements discussed in previous chapters. The preaching of the word held a vital place and helped to lay the doctrinal foundations of our church life. The house-group or cell, meetings were mini congregational meetings but with a strong emphasis on fellowship and pastoral care.

As the church grew, and we gained more understanding of worship, we found ourselves moving into a style of worship meeting where there was a greater emphasis on celebration than participation. The change crept upon us unawares for a number of reasons. With more people packed into the building, vocal contributions from the floor became less and less audible. People often felt intimidated by the size, and so only the brave would venture up to the front of the meeting to prophesy, or exercise other spiritual gifts, with the aid of a microphone. It was during this time that we learned how to celebrate. Following principles from the musical life of David's Tabernacle, singers and musicians gave a strong lead to the worship. There were contrasting times of high praise with much jubilation and times of hushed stillness in the quietness of God's presence.

Participation in these meetings was more corporate than individual. It was then that we realized that the one New Testament meeting that is described, the smaller congregational, or body, meeting of 1 Corinthians 14:26, was the one meeting we were not having. As a result of growth the church divided into two congregations, but even then the Sunday morning worship time was more of a celebration than a congregation. Recently we have divided into five congregations and this is providing the opportunity to encourage more people to participate in the meeting.

We all meet once a month for a large celebration in a public building in Brighton. This is unashamedly a time of festival, with the worship led by the musicians, and participation is corporate. The dynamics of house-group life are also changing, with a greater emphasis on working out our personal relationships and love for one another rather than the house group being a mini congregational meeting.

If worship includes the way we conduct ourselves in the whole round of life's activities, it is not necessary to have a 'worship time' in a house-group meeting. We worship God in the way we relate to one another in fellowship. Worship then becomes a lifestyle rather than something we always do in a meeting.

In these three types of gathering, then, we have different ways of expressing worship. In the celebration type our model is the Tabernacle of David. In the congregational meeting there are opportunities for all to participate as we minister to one another (1 Cor 14:26; Col 3:16; Eph 5:18). The smaller cell gatherings are for discipleship and caring for one another, yet another way in which we can worship God.

As we are learning about these different meetings, we are finding that we have to consider how we structure our meetings and how the worship is led. Celebration, congregation and cells are implicit in Scripture as a basis for gathering. Each church, commensurate with its size, can structure its meetings accordingly. A church of a hundred people meeting regularly should beware of leading worship from the front as in a celebration. A large church of several hundred should be aware of the need to provide a setting for a body meeting. Attention needs to be given to the purpose and dynamics of each meeting.

9

The Worship Musicians

Praise and worship involve more than congregational singing. Traditionally the organ and the piano have been the prominent instruments for congregational accompaniment, but the Bible encourages a much greater variety of instruments:

> Praise Him with trumpet sound;
> Praise Him with harp and lyre.
> Praise Him with timbrel and dancing;
> Praise Him with stringed instruments and pipe.
> Praise Him with loud cymbals;
> Praise Him with resounding cymbals,
> Let everything that has breath praise the Lord!
>
> (Ps 150:3-6).

Woodwind, strings, brass and percussion are all included. The Psalms would have been accompanied by a wide variety of instruments. There are many references to instruments accompanying worship in the Old Testament. In the New Testament the elders in the book of Revelation led the worship accompanied by their instruments (Rev 5:8; 14:2; 15:2).

There are many opportunities for learning musical instruments, and many state schools have peripatetic instrumental teachers. In the 1950s the guitar was popularized, bringing simple but effective music-making into the home. The short-lived 'skiffle' craze gave a great impetus to home music-making. The piano, which was the traditional instrument to learn in the home, was replaced by the guitar which, by the learning of three chords, could give an accompaniment to a simple song without long hours of arduous scale practice. During the early 60s pop music was dominated by the guitar, but as this music became more sophisticated other instruments grew in popularity. Young people not only wanted to listen to pop music but were keen to play in groups and bands. During the early 70s when I was director of music in a comprehensive school, I had over 200 children learning instruments—everything from classical violin to rock guitar. Music became a popular subject when there were opportunities for instrumental tuition.

Many education authorities have made provision for instrumental tuition, and educational music has broken out of its classical-orientated curriculum. There is now, generally, a much greater diversity. This is reflected in the annual schools' 'prom' held in the Albert Hall. It is possible to hear youth symphony orchestras, big bands, rock groups, folk groups, recorder ensembles and choirs all reflecting the wide range of musical tuition available.

This trend is also reflected in the church where many more people are now able to play instruments. Churches need to recognize the gifting in their congregations and use it for the kingdom. Worship is greatly enhanced when there is a variety of instrumental music. The problem is gathering the musicians together and giving them something to play. How do you combine an *ad hoc* number of instruments into a unified blend? A church may find it has a flute, a violin, a guitar, a piano and a trombone. What do you do with them?

Different instruments create different moods and may helpfully illustrate words. They can be used to give accompaniment to prophecy, readings and prophetic songs, and they can

also be used for playing selahs. Worship leaders need to be
aware of the different sounds instruments make and the
contribution they can give to worship. Elders need to
encourage musical gifting and view the musicians not as an
optional extra but as an integral part of the worshipping community. (See appendix 3 for some guidelines to musicians on
how to orchestrate.)

Selahs and prophetic playing

The music group should learn how to develop accompaniment
to worship songs, and see themselves as having a prophetic
role in the worship. Under the guidance of the worship leader,
there should be times when the instruments play on their own
without singing. This is not music for music's sake, or giving a
performance; it is helping to provide the right setting for God
to speak. As we have seen, selahs in the Psalms are generally
understood as pauses for the musicians to play while the
congregation would meditate upon the words of the psalm.
Music can express emotion and provide a background for
meditation. The prophet Elisha once called for a minstrel
before he prophesised.

Music in and of itself is not prophetic because the vital
element of prophecy is God's word. Prophecy has content but
music can release the heart both to prophesy and to receive
prophecy. David was anointed by the Spirit to play music, and
the fact that his playing soothed the troubled Saul shows its
spiritual dimension. God, the creator of music, can use music
when it is played by anointed, creative musicians to prepare
the heart for his word. The reading of Scripture passages with
musical accompaniment interpreting the words, prophecy
with musical background, and playing sensitively in pauses in
the meeting can all help to open the mind and heart. Naturally, carefulness is needed. Demonstrations of skill have no
place, neither has music for music's sake.

Worship at David's Tabernacle was full of musical creativity
and vitality. During the musicians' rehearsals it is helpful to

spend time playing together and improvising some music around a passage of Scripture. Players should learn to listen and respond. Perhaps a simple repetitive chord structure could provide a basis for the improvisation. Playing for singing in the spirit requires sensitivity. There are different aspects to singing in the spirit which need to be understood by the musicians. Spontaneous bursts and also quiet times of singing in tongues require little accompaniment. The emphasis should be placed on the singing. There are times when the musicians can give encouragement to singing in the spirit by taking an instrumental lead. In a quiet, gentle time of singing in the spirit a melodic instrument could perhaps weave a simple melodic line, while in more triumphant moments the brass could make proclamations with fanfares.

Songs of response between the worship leader, the musicians and the congregation can be most effective. For example, over a sustained chord:

Worship leader:	'Let all the people lift up their voices to God.'
Congregation:	Respond by all singing.
Worship leader:	'Let the trumpets sound a fanfare for the King.'
Orchestra:	Trumpets respond with a brief fanfare.
Worship leader:	'Let the people shout joyfully to God.'
Congregation:	Joyful shouting (musicians keep playing).
Worship leader:	'Let all the instruments of music and all the people together make a joyful noise unto the Lord.'
Congregation and musicians:	All join in the response.

Musicians have a vital ministry in a church that is seeking to be a worshipping people. They are not an optional extra to make the worship more interesting. The musical priests in the Old Testament had a definite calling and appointing to the task. They had a role in leading the people in praise and worship. Elders need to see the importance of the musicians, spending time with them, encouraging and teaching them, and releasing them to function.

The musicians' character

Musical gifting is not enough to be a worship musician. There is an awesome responsibility in giving a lead to a congregation, and so character and gifting must go together. The young David was described as 'a skillful musician, a mighty man of valor, a warrior, one prudent in speech, and a handsome man; and the Lord is with him' (1 Sam 16:18). He is an excellent character model for all worship musicians.

Skill

Each musician should develop their instrumental playing. Regular practice on improving aural skills, improvisation, stamina and technique will help the musician feel equipped. Never settle for the standard reached.

Victorious Christian living

David was a mighty man of valour and a warrior, even though he was young. It is not a good idea to allow a young Christian into the worship band. Time to settle into the church and a proven Christian life will help to strengthen them for the inevitable vulnerability that public ministry brings. If a musician is living out the victorious Christian life, they will know how to overcome temptations of pride and ego. A humble spirit is essential.

Prudent in speech

Musicians are prone to be critical. The rehearsal time can bring tensions, differences of opinion, and impatience which can all test relationships. If the musicians do not know how to work together, this will affect the worship: the tensions will be communicated. Speaking lovingly to one another in encouragement and correcting without criticism will help to keep relationships as well as the music harmonious.

Attractive

Being handsome or attractive, as King David is described, is not dependent on external features but on an inner attitude of the heart. Seeing ourselves as God sees us helps us to have a good self-image. Sometimes mistakes are made, or playing isn't as good as it could be, and this can affect a musician's attitude to himself. A constant questioning of one's ability, self-analysis and looking for approval will inhibit the worship musician's service. Effective worship musicians will know who they are in Christ, and their inner attractiveness will affect the way they minister.

Knowing God's presence

A personal relationship with God, just as David had, will help to overcome the problem of worshipping and playing. To give a lead in worship the musician needs to be a worshipper. This is not always easy in a meeting where there is a concentration on playing the right notes in the right key. The best way to overcome this problem is by spending time at home worshipping with an instrument. If we live close to God we can be aware of his presence constantly.

The chief musician

It is helpful if church leaders appoint a chief musician: somebody who takes decisions and generally oversees the music. This role need not necessarily go to the most competent musician, because spiritual maturity and an ability to gather and lead people is a more important qualification for a chief musician. He should relate with the elders and be seen as having a leadership role within the church. Where a church gives worship a high priority the chief musician fulfils a vital function. Co-ordinating, giving pastoral input, relating with the worship leaders, and keeping a control over the musicians in public are all facets of this ministry. The chief musician should be able to draw on other people's musical strengths and allow gifting to emerge. Where a church's musicians are functioning under effective leadership, with the freedom to develop and function in their ministry, that church will find its worship greatly enhanced and will enjoy the blessing of God.

Introducing a singing group

At Clarendon we have found it helpful to have a team of singers working with the instrumental musicians. It is important to remember that a singing group does not exist to perform to the congregation. Singers were given a prominent place in Old Testament worship. They were appointed and set apart in their ministry of song to help give a lead to the congregation. In a body meeting there may not be a need for a specialized singing group, except to teach new songs and help the congregation pick up on a song that has started from the floor. It is in the setting of a celebration that a singing group comes into its own, supporting the worship leader, leading the congregation, and being free to move out in prophetic song. It may be helpful to write vocal arrangements of songs, or allow the singers themselves to extemporize parts. But this requires careful attention to phrasing and chording, as well as the voicing of the parts.

Prophetic singing

Prophetic singing, sometimes called the 'song of the Lord', is where somebody sings out prophetic truth in the form of a solo voice. It may be over a sustained chord or sequence of chords. When singing a prophetic song, keep within the vocal limitations of the voice. Sometimes excitement and adrenalin can replace genuine anointing, and the voice tries to reach notes hitherto unattainable. Those who minister in prophetic song can practise by singing Scripture. Personally I love to sing Scripture. It helps me to retain it in my mind and develop the gift of prophetic singing.

Prophetic singing often needs pruning. A good opening may move on in a formless or repetitive fashion. To prevent this, try to formulate phrases in the mind before they are sung out, and try to crystallize the essence of the prophetic song into a brief statement. Singing a new song to the Lord can bring a worship time into revelation and release. It is a significant ministry and singers need to learn how to wait on God for prophetic utterance, and develop their singing technique to give full expression to the truth they are seeking to convey.

Use of P.A.

We live in a technological age where P.A. systems and microphones are becoming much more commonplace. Church buildings were originally designed with good live acoustics suitable for an unamplified voice. Singing and chanting the liturgy helped to carry the words where speech would have been inaudible. Today the situation is different.

P.A. systems can be both a help and a hindrance. The most important thing is that people can hear what is going on. In a congregational meeting the less P.A. the better, and if musicians, singers and speakers paid more attention to voice projection then the perpetual need for amplification would be modified. I once heard Segovia play in the packed 2,300-seater Brighton Dome. Every note on his nylon string unamplified guitar was clear. An unamplified flute solo can carry across the sound of a full orchestra in a Tchaikovsky symphony. If speakers, singers and players learned about breath control and projection many of their acoustic problems would be solved. The use of a microphone in a body meeting can inhibit contribution and halt the flow of the meeting. Use as little as possible, providing everyone is heard.

A celebration needs a P.A. system with a good mixing

console. The P.A. team need to be thought of as an integral part of the musical team and need the same kind of covering and care as the musicians. Church leaders need to be aware of this because in human terms the person operating the mixing desk has a certain control over the meeting. It is vital that the P.A. team know exactly what the musicians and speaker desire, and mix the console accordingly. They should be aware of the musicians' need to hear what they are playing: clarity is more important than volume. A well-mixed P.A. in a celebration will give a body of sound that the congregation will respond to. Worship leader, singers, instrumentalists and P.A. team need to learn to work as one team to help create the right environment for the people of God to worship.

10

Leading Worship

With the applause of the large audience ringing in my ears, my dream seemed like being fulfilled. I had just conducted my own composition in one of the leading concert halls on the south coast of England: a cantata for rock group, symphony orchestra and choir. The composition was hailed as a breakthrough in the fusion of jazz, rock and classical music, and drew the attention of the media and a leading record company. The realization of my one ambition, to become a successful composer, seemed to be on the way.

The call of God has a remarkable way of disrupting our ambitions, and I now find myself in the Christian ministry. In response to the call of God, I not only gave up my ambition, I also completely submitted my musical abilities to him. I had no inclination of the way God would give back both the gift and the desire to make music.

Having had a formal musical training, and being involved in conducting, I had some important lessons to learn when I began to lead worship. The art of orchestral conducting is getting other people to play well, according to the interpretation of the music that is in the mind of the conductor. Dressed splendidly in white tie and tail-coat, conductors often act out their interpretation of the music with energy and flamboyance. But is this really necessary? I recently watched a TV programme about a conductor's masterclass. Four aspiring young conductors were being trained by Zubin Mehta. He made a very telling comment to one young trainee who had been practising his movements in a mirror. He told him that all the clever theatrical movements may look good on the podium with a well-trained orchestra, but if he could not make the orchestra play in time then he might as well not be there. The art of conducting is to draw the very best out of an orchestra. Sir Adrian Boult only had to touch his moustache and the orchestra would suddenly crescendo. He hardly moved a muscle as his precise and accurate beat produced some truly memorable performances. How different from the histrionics and gyrations of some conductors who put up a very good performance themselves.

The first thing I had to learn about leading worship was that the worship leader is not there to perform and draw attention to himself, but like a good conductor he will seek to give a lead as unobtrusively as possible. The ministry of the worship leader is not mentioned in any of the list of ministries in the New Testament, but it is possible that Paul had this ministry in mind, among others, when he says in Romans 12:8 that he who leads should do so with diligence. The Greek word for 'leads' here is *pro-istamenos* which means to stand before. The role of the worship leader is to stand before the meeting to help and guide the worship.

Qualities of a worship leader

1. Submission

During the days of David's Tabernacle there were many musicians. Chenaniah, Asaph, Heman and Jeduthun had a leadership role. They exercised their ministry under the direction of King David. In the local church situation it is the elders who have responsibility for overseeing all aspects of church life, including the worship time. This is particularly important in an open worship time with contributions. Prophecies need to be weighed and everything should be done in a decent and orderly fashion.

However, the elders may not have the ability to lead the congregation in thanksgiving, praise and worship. And so the appointment of a gifted worship leader is important. He needs to remain humbly submitted to the elders who in turn need to recognize gifting and encourage this ministry to emerge.

2. Worshipful

The most effective way to lead worship is to be a worshipper. Leading by example is much more effective than exhortations to 'raise the roof' or 'let's all jump for joy'. Worship is for God's pleasure, not to create an atmosphere. Sometimes congregations are slow to respond, but cajoling or condemning will not produce the desired result. The good worship leader will draw the people, not drive them. Focusing on some aspect of truth can capture people's imaginations and lift their hearts towards God in adoration. But driving the people with exhortations will be counter-productive. People may begin to sing, dance and shout, but their hearts may not be really worshipping. If the people still fail to respond, the best thing the worship leader can do is to fix his attention on God very consciously and worship. If there is any life at all in the people, they will soon follow.

3. Preparation

Times of worship do not normally just happen. While there should always be room for spontaneity, there should also be a framework in which the worship time takes place. The Psalms are poems with structure and shape; God is a God of order and form. Preparation, therefore, is essential. The worship leader should prepare his own heart, develop his skills, and make sure that each meeting he is responsible for is adequately prepared. Diligence in the development of skills will help the congregation to feel secure in the leader.

A thorough knowledge of worship songs is essential. Songs old and new need to be learned and absorbed. Compile a loose-leaf folder with a flexible indexing system. Record each song with its key signature and categorize them under different headings. For example:

Songs of joyful praise.
Songs about God's character.
Songs about God's workings.
Songs which express something to God.
Songs which express something to one another.
Songs which exalt Jesus.
Intimate, quiet love songs.
Prophetic truth in song.
Testimony and experience songs.
Songs of the kingdom.
Our life in God together.
The atonement.
Spiritual warfare.

Within these categories (there could be many more) there may be songs that are particularly appropriate for starting a meeting or for responding to an appeal or to one another. With such information readily available, the worship leader need never be taken unawares in a meeting.

Scripture references for each song help undergird the truths that the song is declaring. A sense of progression from one song to another is helpful, so song groupings can be prepared on a particular theme. The diligent worship leader will also be prepared by being aware of the latest new worship songs available on recordings and in music books.

Preparation to lead a worship meeting is best undertaken in private worship times. The way God meets with the worship leader in the secret place will have repercussions in the public meeting. Spending time alone in worship, meditating on the word, reading about others' experiences of God, a thorough acquaintance with the repertoire of worship songs, old and new, and a working knowledge of our heritage of hymns will all help the worship leader feel well prepared.

4. Communication

Communicating with elders, musicians and the congregation is an essential aspect of leading worship. Musicians may occupy a vulnerable position in a worship meeting because there is often an unpredictability as to what may happen. Communicating with the musicians well in advance of the start of the meeting will help them to feel more prepared and instil confidence. Searching for the right key or feverishly turning the pages of several song books to find a long-forgotten, obscure chorus can present many practical difficulties for musicians. The instrumentalists need to know of anything unusual that may happen so they can practise and be adequately prepared.

If an overhead projector is used, make sure that the acetates you need for that particular meeting are available, and always carry spare pens and acetates around. Make sure that the operator of the overhead projector knows which songs are intended to be used. This sounds obvious, but it is amazing what can be overlooked if you are not organized. A means of communication needs to be developed between the worship leader and the musicians. Is the song going to be repeated? Do we have the last verse again? Simple hand signals operated as unobtrusively as possible can help the worship leader and the musicians to communicate. It is also helpful to the elders if worship leaders communicate their thoughts and aspirations for any meeting they may be leading.

5. Sensitivity

I once stood on a mountainside in Wales and watched a pair of buzzards rise higher and higher until they were tiny specks in the sky. I was intrigued by the way these magnificent birds of prey gained height. They hardly flapped their enormous wings, but as they stretched them out they caught the air thermals which caused them to rise up and up. It all looked so effortless.

A worship meeting can operate on the same principle. It is not a matter of how much effort everybody puts into the meeting, but how much sensitivity there is to the Holy Spirit. There looms a danger of disjointedness when contributions flow without any reference to each other. A song, a prophecy, another song, a word of knowledge, a prayer, another song, followed by singing in the spirit, a testimony and yet another song. The meeting may appear to be alive with contributions but lacking in any sense of progression.

The worship leader needs to be sensitive to what the Holy Spirit is doing, and not move on until he moves on. Rather like the buzzard, there needs to be a riding of the thermals of the Holy Spirit. Contributions and songs should flow in harmony, creating a sense of unity in the meeting. However, just as a sudden gust of wind can affect the flight of the bird, so a sudden and unexpected blowing of the Holy Spirit can change the orientation of a meeting. When God moves in this way, perhaps through a prophecy or a particular anointing on a song, it can be exhilarating. When the worship leader is changing the direction every few minutes it can be very frustrating.

A classic mistake that is easily made is that worship leaders can participate too much. The beginning of a meeting is always a sensitive time. It is not the moment for preaching sermons, even short ones, for this can merely frustrate a congregation that is ready to worship.

A simple seed-thought to focus people's minds on God should be enough to lead them into thanksgiving and praise. Neither is there any need for homilies between each song. The sensitive worship leader will allow the meeting to flow.

Sensitivity is a skill which needs to be practised. Learn to listen to the voice of the Holy Spirit, and keep in tune with what he is saying and doing in a meeting. The key is to be relaxed. If the worship leader is edgy, constantly wondering what to do next, and for ever jumping in with comments, the flow of the meeting will become stilted. Relax, do not be afraid to wait, and move on when the Spirit leads.

6. Confidence

Displays of skill and the ability to lead people should have no place in the life of the worship leader, but confidence exercised humbly will help a congregation to feel secure. Never give instructions that are impossible to follow. It is no good exhorting a congregation to march around the room singing if the song is not known, or encouraging them to dance if there is not enough leg room. The worship leader should have an awareness of his surroundings and the abilities of his congregation. Simple instructions clearly conveyed will meet a ready response. Pray for the meeting that is to be led; pray for the people; pray for the musicians, and pray that God will come and delight himself in the praises of his people.

7. Appropriate forms of worship

The worship leader needs to be aware of different types of meeting and lead the worship accordingly. Is the meeting a celebration? Is it a congregational meeting with contributions? Is there going to be breaking of bread? Will unsaved people be present?

The good worship leader will give attention to the purpose of each meeting. Many of the trends in worship are influenced by what happens at major Christian events such as Spring Harvest and Downs and Dales Bible Weeks. Thousands of people attend these events, necessitating a very prominent lead in the worship. The worship leader will begin the worship. He will encourage people to sing, dance, raise their hands, and sing in the spirit. He may well sing prophetically. His role is to steer the meeting. He knows which songs to sing, and he will bring things to a definite conclusion. This is a perfectly valid way of leading a large gathering: it makes the congregation feel secure, the musicians have confidence, and it provides a platform for the ministry of the word. However, leading a celebration is not the same as leading worship in a congregation. To copy a worship leader who is leading thousands, and apply his model in a congregation of a hundred, will actually inhibit the flow of body ministry.

Leading a celebration

Standing before a large crowd of people to lead them in praise
and worship is both awesome and exciting, especially when
they have a strong desire to worship. The worship leader can
feel as though he is at the controls of an extremely powerful
racing-car. One touch of the throttle and all the latent power
underneath the bonnet is unleashed in a burst of acceleration.
The driver needs to harness and control the power at his
fingertips; he must know when to brake, when to accelerate,
and when to change gear. The racing-car driver will time
things to perfection to gain maximum performance combined
with safety.

The leader of a celebration must recognize the latent power
in a large congregation of worshippers. His job is to gather the
people and harness that power. I am not suggesting that the
worship leader should control and manipulate, but under the
guidance of the Holy Spirit encourage the worship that is
already in the hearts of the people to be released. He must be
able to channel exuberant praise, giving a definite and firm
lead to both congregation and musicians alike. Leading a
celebration needs sensitivity to the Holy Spirit, a prophetic
anointing, a clear musical gift, and an ability to lead confidently a large number of people.

1. Sensitivity to the Holy Spirit

There is a natural exuberance in a large crowd of people singing together. Excitement and emotions can run high, but such
fervour on its own should not be mistaken for the presence of
God. The worship leader needs to keep the attention of the
people focused on God. Hand raising, dancing, singing,
shouting and joyful applause should arise from praising,
thankful hearts and be directed towards God. Participating in
these external expressions to liven up the meeting or to create
an atmosphere is quite wrong. God is a God of emotion and
he wants us to express our emotions, but what we feel springs
from what we know. Having our hearts and minds directed

towards God, and praising the Lord with understanding, will help us to release our bodies in worship. There is no place for such songs as 'If you want joy you must jump for it'. Such banal sentiments have no place in worship that is in spirit and in truth.

The worship leader needs to be sensitive to the Holy Spirit so that the people are led in spirit and in truth, not by carnally stirring up their emotions. Sensitivity to the Holy Spirit while leading a large gathering comes by the worship leader himself focusing on God, but also by being aware of what God is doing among the people. If he is so taken up with God that he becomes totally unaware of the congregation, without first having gathered them to God, then they will find it difficult to respond and follow. On the other hand, if he is completely taken up with the congregation he will become nervous and be constantly wondering what to do next.

Leading a celebration is like conducting an orchestra. The conductor draws music from the players, keeps them in time, and helps to interpret the music. The worship leader gathers the people to God, and as he worships so he takes the people with him, occasionally giving guidance, occasionally encouraging. Just as the good conductor allows his players to play, so the worship leader allows the people to worship. A sensitive leader will know when to encourage, when to exhort, and when to remain silent. This sensitivity is developed by maintaining a consistent walk with God.

2. Prophetic anointing

Worship in a celebration provides a setting for a corporate prophetic declaration. When the congregation of Israel gathered to worship with psalms at David's Tabernacle, there was a strong emphasis on the declaration of God's purpose. We have already discussed the prophetic nature of the Psalms and the prophetic nature of God's people. It is when we celebrate that we have the opportunity to declare corporately the purposes of God.

The leaders of worship at David's Tabernacle were not only

prophets themselves, but they also led the people in prophetic worship:

> Moreover, David and the commanders of the army set apart for the service some of the sons of Asaph and of Heman and of Jeduthun, who were to prophesy with lyres, harps, and cymbals . . . . The sons of Asaph . . . were under the direction of Asaph, who prophesied under the direction of the king. . . . The sons of Jeduthun . . . prophesied in giving thanks and praising the Lord. . . . All these were the sons of Heman the king's seer to exalt him according to the words of God. . . . All these were under the direction of their father to sing in the house of the Lord, with cymbals, harps and lyres, for the service of the house of God. Asaph, Jeduthun and Heman were under the direction of the king (1 Chron 25:1-6).

To lead a celebration effectively there needs to be an understanding of the purposes of God in this generation. What people sing both reflects and shapes what they believe. Therefore the choice of songs should be based on what God is currently saying. Of course, God's word is timeless and all of it is relevant, but there are seasons when God focuses the attention of his church on a particular aspect of the truth. Over recent years there has been a recovery of neglected truths as God has been restoring the church, and often worship songwriters around the world have been quickened by a particular theme without realizing what was happening. Songs about building the church, songs of the reign of Christ and the establishing of his kingdom, songs about spiritual warfare, and songs about our fellowship in Christ seem to have come in waves.

The leader of a celebration should not only understand what God is currently saying, and reflect this in the choice of songs, but he should also be able to give a lead in prophesying, particularly in song. Chenaniah was not only a prophetic leader, he was also skilled in singing. To lead a celebration requires a certain amount of musical ability. A good clear voice, the ability to hold the melody line without going out of tune, and the ability to confidently pitch a song are essential.

It is not helpful to a congregation if the leader experiments with vocal harmonies or cannot sing in tune. A good clear melodic lead is essential. This does not mean that the worship leader has to be a trained musician, but he should have an innate musical ability.

The musicians themselves have a key role in leading celebrations, and the leaders should know how to communicate with them. Practise the songs with the musicians to get the speed and feel of the song right. It is helpful for the worship leader to have regular worship times with the musicians, developing extemporary prophetic singing and playing. This will have repercussions in the public meeting with musicians and worship leader flowing together.

3. Confident leading

The worship leader sets the tone for the meeting; he needs to give a confident lead from the moment he stands on his feet. It is a good idea to think out an introductory sentence. Standing before a large number of people can have a numbing effect on the mind. Be clear and precise in giving instructions, but be warm in gathering people. Relax, and make people feel relaxed. Be aware of the practical problems of leading a large congregation. Time-lag in a hall with bad acoustics can sound like an out-of-phase stereo and make it difficult for people to keep together. Do not allow the indiscriminate tambourine bashers to dictate the tempo. A simple hand motion in time to the music can help keep the musicians and congregation in time, although conducting should be done sparingly and only when necessary. When it is overdone, it draws attention to the worship leader.

The form of the celebration

The biggest problem in leading a celebration is keeping a sense of flow. Because the leading of a celebration comes from the front, the leader needs to know how to move on from one part of the worship to the next as unobtrusively as possible. The biggest mistake is talking too much between songs, leaving the people listening to the worship leader instead of worshipping God. It is helpful to think of the worship in three sections: thanksgiving and praise, worship and celebration.

Find songs in each section that link together and move on from one song to another. The link should be based on a combination of the truth expressed and the musical style. Finding two or three linking songs in each of these sections can create a flow, and only the occasional comment is necessary. This allows the people to worship. Singing songs several times, singing half the song again, slowing down the tempo, singing in the spirit, and returning to the original song help people to meditate on the truth that the songs are expressing.

There is a time to move on from praise into worship. Intimacy with God should be an integral part of a worship time. An unhurried waiting, a gentle love song, and a quiet instrumental selah are all helpful ways of coming to 'kiss the King'. Worship is an affair of the heart, and there needs to be times in celebration worship where the soul's longing and thirsting after God is both expressed and met.

A sample of a structure for a celebration

Section 1

'I will enter His gates with thanksgiving in my heart.'
    'Sing praises unto God, sing praises.'
    'Almighty God, we bring You praise.'
    'God of glory, we exalt Your name.'

If the musicians are prepared, each song can run into another, thus moving progressively to a place where worship can be expressed.

Section 2

'Open your eyes, see the glory of the King.'
    'I worship You, Almighty God.'
    'Jesus You are the radiance of the Father's glory.'

Section 3

'For this purpose Christ was revealed.'

This final song brings a sense of proclamation and going out.

The above is only a guideline to show how song groupings can help a meeting to flow rather than become stilted with endless commentaries on the songs to be sung. Within this structure allow for spontaneity of expression from the musicians, as well as prophetic song and singing in the spirit.

The leader of a celebration should be aware of what God wants to say and do in a particular meeting, and should have this in mind. Having presented some structural principles governing a celebration, the worship leader and the musicians should be free to let God interrupt and do whatever he wants. Sometimes there is an element of unpredictability in the operation of the Spirit and we must be careful not to invent forms of worship that do not allow for this spontaneous activity.

If the worship leader has a sense of form and order as a guideline, it will help him to feel secure in his leadership. This is also biblical as the Psalms have form and structure. As the worship leader prepares, there is no reason why the form and structure cannot be invaded by the Holy Spirit. If preachers can prepare beforehand, so can worship leaders. And just as preachers can break off from their notes under the inspiration of the Spirit, so can worship leaders. Worship in a celebration should have a form and structure which the Holy Spirit uses. If he then disposes with the structure and does something completely different, then the worship leader needs to be in tune with him so that he doesn't get in the way of God. Leading a celebration is an awesome and thrilling ministry.

Leading a congregation

Leading a congregational meeting with contributions needs a totally different approach from leading a celebration. The leader of a congregational meeting could be likened to a punter on a river. The momentum of the river actually carries the punt and its occupants downstream. The punter will give a little push to start the punt off, projecting into the river's current, but then the pole is used to steer around bends, keeping the craft on course.

In a congregational meeting the impetus comes from the people rather than the worship leader. People are free to start songs, prophesy and exercise other spiritual gifts. It is the kind of meeting described in 1 Corinthians 14:26—'When you assemble, each one has a psalm, has a teaching, has a revelation, has a tongue, has an interpretation. Let all things be done for edification.' The worship leader is there to keep the meeting on course, gathering what others are bringing and helping to keep the meeting moving in the right direction. A good congregational meeting not only needs a good worship leader but a congregation who are willing to participate. Church elders need to exercise oversight by teaching on the subject of the body meeting and bringing the necessary shape to the gatherings.

The key to leading a body meeting is its beginning. It needs to open with a definite focus. A body meeting can begin in a similar way to a celebration, with a progression of songs on the theme of thanksgiving and praise. This needs preparation and discussion with the musicians. From his point, however the meeting should run more freely than a celebration. In a good body meeting, with contributions flowing, the worship leader will not have to do anything else until the end of the worship time. This does not mean that he remains passive. He should be aware of the principles outlined in leading a celebration, because a good body meeting will have a similar structure and form: thanksgiving and praise, worship and celebration. The people need to be taught this structure and form and be aware which stage the meeting has reached before a contribution is made. Having both the mind and the timing of the Holy Spirit will cause contributions to be in the flow of what God is doing. A body meeting can become disjointed if people do not listen to what has just taken place. Each contribution should arise out of what has just happened (remember the illustration of the buzzard).

The essential difference between a celebration and a congregation are:

Celebration	Congregation
The leader prepares all the songs.	The leader prepares the first two or three songs.
The leader steers the meeting and says what will happen next.	The congregation dictates what happens next by its contributions.
Only a selected gifted few participate publicly.	All may participate publicly.

Leading a congregational meeting is difficult because of its unpredictability, therefore the congregation needs to be confident that the worship leader will lead effectively, bringing a sense of harmony and order to the meeting. Contributions that are not brought from the Holy Spirit, verbosity and sing-alongs all need careful correction. The art of leading a congregational meeting needs to be developed if the church is to be a functioning priesthood. When congregational worship leaders copy the leaders of celebrations they will frustrate worship and body ministry. A congregational worship leader needs all the qualities and skills of a celebration leader, but with the added ingredient of the kind of sensitivity which instinctively knows when to interject and when to remain silent.

Celebrations and congregations both have their place in God's purpose for gathering people to worship. Their similarities and their differences need to be observed in order for people to minister to God and one another with maximum effectiveness.

11

Praise and the Kingdom

The streets of London, late at night, had an atmosphere of foreboding, with their barred and shuttered shop-fronts and rubbish strewn all over the pavements. There was a stark contrast between the outside world and the inside of the minibus.

The young people from a church in Basingstoke had been regularly travelling into London to rehearse for a production of *Come Together*, the musical by Jimmy and Carol Owens. On this particular night, the laughing, singing, happy group of youngsters could have had no idea of the events awaiting them.

Through the environs of London, onto the M4 and then off onto the Reading road, they headed for home. The route was familiar enough. Just as the minibus turned onto the Reading road, a car forced them into a lay-by. A menacing gang tried to break in, one of them standing on the running-board and declaring evil intentions to the occupants.

What happened next may surprise you. The young people in the minibus began to worship the Lord, singing and praising in tongues. The effect was not immediate, but gradually the gang left and the minibus arrived home safely. An ugly and potentially vicious situation had been defused by the power of God. Through the praises of the young people, and, significantly, through the prayers of two of the wives in Basingstoke who had suddenly felt that the minibus was in danger, God's presence was released into the situation. Satan is dethroned wherever God is enthroned.

Praise and the establishing of God's kingdom is a major theme running through the book of Psalms. It points to the coming of Jesus and the establishing of the kingdom through his life and ministry. Jesus proclaimed the good news that the kingdom of God had come. The sick were healed, demons were cast out, and the poor heard the gospel preached.

After Pentecost, the Apostles continued to preach the kingdom, demonstrating its power by healing the sick and bringing deliverance to the demonized. As churches were established and new communities of believers were formed, the kingdom of God was seen not as an abstract concept or just a future hope: it was a reality in people's lives as they came under the rule and authority of King Jesus. Paul describes the change salvation brings in terms of leaving one kingdom and entering another: 'For He delivered us from the domain of darkness, and transferred us to the kingdom of His beloved Son, in whom we have redemption, the forgiveness of sins' (Col 1:13-14).

To be a citizen of the kingdom of God means a totally alternative way of living. It affects our character—we live by the principles of God's word. Jesus gave a manifesto of kingdom living in his sermon on the mount. The gospel means that the human heart can be so changed by the grace of God that a person can live according to these standards—that is the miracle of our new life in Christ. Living in the kingdom means not losing your temper or feeling resentment. It means loving your neighbour as you love yourself. It means husbands loving their wives as Christ loved the church, and wives submitting to their husbands. The kingdom of God is a very down-to-earth place to live. At the heart of living in the kingdom is loving submission to the King. Loving God with our whole heart, mind, soul and strength; honouring Jesus and giving him glory in everything, and constantly being filled with the power of the Holy Spirit.

When the Psalmist declares that God is 'enthroned upon the praises of Israel' (Ps 22:3), he is referring to the people of God acknowledging the rule of God in their declarations of praise. The throne of God is established and his rule cannot be thwarted by anything—he sovereignly rules in the universe he has created. And yet, paradoxically, as the people of God bring their praises they enthrone him. It is a paradox, too, that God's presence is everywhere, and yet as we worship, enthroning him on our praises, his presence is released. Yet another paradox is that Jesus has defeated Satan, the kingdom is established, and yet the church has a mandate to bring in the kingdom.

The kingdom of God is an everlasting kingdom that cannot be shaken. Through our redemption we have become citizens of this kingdom and participants in establishing its rule over the kingdom of darkness. We bring in the kingdom by evangelism, by our life and character, and by praise and worship. Evangelism proclaims the truth of the kingdom to those in darkness; our life and character testifies of the power of the kingdom, and praise and worship establishes the kingdom in the hearts of its citizens as they live in total God-consciousness. Praise and worship also declares to God what he loves to hear from those who love him. Principalities and powers also hear the praises of God's people, and tremble.

When the young people in the minibus began to praise the Lord, praise became a weapon against the Enemy. The fact that praise overcame fear showed the God-consciousness of those young people. God was enthroned on their praises and he delivered them. Another example of praise as a weapon comes from a story about my grandfather. He was converted as a young man in Victorian England, and entered the Salvation Army training college in Clapton, London. He became a Salvation Army officer in Booth's Army, and his diaries contain thrilling stories of the exploits of the Army in those early years of its history, when its aggressive evangelism saw thousands converted.

One day, with another army officer, he visited a young girl suffering from tuberculosis, a disease which was fatal in those days. The girl was in her bedroom and when her mother told her that the two Salvation Army officers had come to visit her she immediately began to scream, cursing and swearing with a vitriolic stream of invectives. Nothing could pacify her. She did not want a pastoral visit or prayer. She wanted to curse God and die.

The two men of God began to worship. Quietly they began to sing, 'Grace there is my every debt to pay, blood to wash my every sin away, power to keep me spotless day by day, for me, for me.' They repeated this song over and over again. Gradually the girl began to calm down, and then she began to sob uncontrollably. Eventually they were able to speak to her, leading her to Jesus. The spiritual stronghold in this girl was broken by the power of God as the two men lifted their hearts and voices in worship.

The kingdom of God is a spiritual kingdom, and so its aggressive confrontation with the kingdom of darkness is a spiritual one. Paul describes this warfare:

> Put on the full armor of God, that you may be able to stand firm against the schemes of the devil. For our struggle is not against flesh and blood, but against the rulers, against the powers, against the world forces of this darkness, against the spiritual forces of wickedness in the heavenly places (Eph 6:11-17).

The Psalms are not only songs of praise, they contain many declarations of war against the enemies of the kingdom:

> I love Thee, O Lord, my strength.
>   The Lord is my rock and my fortress
>   and my deliverer,
> My God, my rock, in whom I take refuge;
>   My shield and the horn of my salvation,
>   my stronghold.
> I call upon the Lord, who is worthy
>   to be praised,

And I am saved from my enemies . . . .
The Lord lives, and blessed be my rock;
  And exalted be the God of my salvation.
The God who executes vengeance for me,
  And subdues peoples under me.
He delivers me from my enemies;
  Surely Thou dost lift me above those who rise
  up against me;
Thou dost rescue me from the violent man.
  Therefore I will give thanks to Thee
  among the nations, O Lord,
And I will sing praises to Thy name.
  He gives great deliverance to His king,
And shows lovingkindness to His anointed,
  To David and his descendants forever (Ps 18:1-3, 46-50).

The enemies that David refers to in the Psalms are a type of the spiritual enemy which the church has to face today, and which Paul describes in Ephesians 6. The Christian life is a constant battleground. Christians are opposed by the world and by Satan as he seeks to rob us in our relationship with God by fear, anxiety and unbelief.

In his book, *I Believe in Satan's Downfall* (London, Hodder and Stoughton, 1981) Michael Green gives a full study on the wiles and strategy of the Enemy:

Satan himself is called a slanderer, the tempter (Matthew 4:3). The dragon and serpent (Revelation 9:11), the prince of the power of the air (Ephesians 2:2), Beelzebub (or lord of the flies) (Matthew 10:25), the ruler of this world (John 12:31) and the evil one.

Satan is strong, he assails men's hearts with lust, pride and hatred. He assails their bodies with disease, torture and death. He assails the institutions of men with structural evil in the realm of politics and education. He manipulates nations (Daniel 10), city councils (1 Thessalonians 2:18), rioting mobs (John 8:44-59) and the elements (Mark 4:39).

He has a hierarchy of angelic beings working out his purpose, principalities, powers, dominions, thrones, names, princes, lords, gods, angels, spirits, unclean spirits, wicked spirits, and elemental spirits.

This wicked hierarchy of evil is an army which is seeking to thwart God's purpose, from world systems right down to individuals. When we become Christians we become conscious of a battle—for the mind, the emotions, the body and the will. Demons will oppress and harrass, and in some cases will cause possession (although it is more accurate to describe someone as being demonized rather than as being possessed). The purpose of this evil army is to usurp God's authority. Satan will do all he can to rob us of what is rightfully ours. There will be confrontational temptations to sin. Fear, loss of peace, and slavery to past bondages are all snares set by him.

Although Satan is strong, he is defeated, and Paul shows us how we can be victorious over his wiles. The passage describing the full armour of God teaches us how we can have victory against the Enemy. The study of this armour is a subject in itself, and the believer would do well to read such books as *The Christian Soldier* (Edinburgh, Banner of Truth, 1977) and *The Christian Warfare* by Dr Martyn Lloyd-Jones (Edinburgh, Banner of Truth 1976). The key to our victory against Satan and his minions is that we understand what Christ has done for us and who we are in him. The armour is picture language which describes the truth of our salvation.

How we stand in victory

1. By being filled with the Spirit

'Be strong in the Lord, and in the strength of His might' (Eph 6:10).

The word 'strong' in Greek comes from the same root as the word used for 'power' in Acts 1:8—'You shall receive power when the Holy Spirit has come upon you.' This word is *dunamis* from which we get such words as 'dynamic' and 'dynamite'. There is a strength which God supplies by his Spirit. We will never overcome the Enemy by will-power or striving but by drawing on the Spirit of God within us.

2. By being clothed with the full armour of God

(a) *Loins girded with truth*. We answer the accusations of the Enemy by the word of God. When Jesus was tempted, he quoted Scripture at Satan. When temptation comes our way, the best way to resist is to declare what God says.

(b) *Breastplate of righteousness*. We have been given righteousness as a gift. Nothing can take it away from us. When a fiery dart comes bringing condemnation, it hits the breastplate of righteousness.

(c) *Feet shod with the preparation of the gospel of peace*. We can be overcomers by being witnesses—witnessing to the gospel actually strengthens us.

(d) *Shield of faith*. However much we are accused, faith in God's word will keep us in victory. To live by faith means that we live by what God says.

(e) *The helmet of salvation*. The helmet covers the head, the part of our body which contains our thinking faculty. Our minds need to be girded with the facts of salvation.

(f) *The sword of the Spirit which is the word of God*. The sword is the only part of the battle-dress that is used as an offensive weapon. The rest of the armour is used for defence and protection. The preaching of God's word is a way of attacking the Enemy. Preaching the gospel and personal evangelism brings the revelation of God's word to those in the kingdom of darkness. Preaching the truth to Christians instructs them in how to live and how to remain in the freedom of their salvation. Jesus said, 'You shall know the truth, and the truth shall make you free' (Jn 8:32). Effective evangelism is not based on persuasive arguments but the proclamation of the Spirit-breathed word of God.

3. By praise and worship

Praise which declares truth strengthens us. The content of what we declare to God in praise helps us to grow in faith. Proclaiming truths about God, our salvation, and the ways of God are a strong weapon against the Enemy. Songs of praise and worship should never be superficial in their content. Singing about God's faithfulness, love and mercy strengthens us in those truths. Singing about our righteousness, God's election of us, our eternal security, and our sonship, establishes these truths like buttresses and will hold fast in temptation or when we don't feel that God is with us. God's word does not change, and singing his word in praise engenders faith.

The prophetic purposes of God can also be declared in song. With so much fear and anxiety in the world, the Christian has a confidence in the destiny God has planned. Fear of the future cannot find a place in the heart and mind of the person confidently declaring God's purpose. Praise strengthens us individually against the wiles of the Enemy. Some of the great hymns are excellent ways of expressing truth to God:

> Immortal invisible, God only wise,
> In light inaccessible hid from our eyes,
> Most blessed, most glorious, the Ancient of Days,
> Almighty, victorious, Thy great name we praise.
>
> Walter Chalmers Smith

> Before the throne of God above
> I have a strong, a perfect plea;
> A great High Priest,
> Whose name is Love,
> Who ever lives and pleads for me.
>
> Charitie Lees Bancroft

Praise and spiritual warfare

> Let the high praises of God be in their mouth,
>   And a two-edged sword in their hand,
> To execute vengeance on the nations,
>   And punishment on the peoples;
> To bind their kings with chains,
>   And their nobles with fetters of iron;
> To execute on them the judgment written (Ps 149:6-9).

Accompanying the two-edged sword are the high praises of God. As the preaching of the word goes forth in proclamation of the kingdom, so the high praises of God declare the truths of the kingdom in singing, dancing, shouting and all the other ways in which God has commanded praise. We have a mandate to execute the victory of Christ as we bring in the kingdom. The word of God, the two-edged sword, is the offensive weapon against the Enemy. The praises on the lips of the saints help keep their focus on God, so they remember that the battle is the Lord's.

We need to beware of confusing the sword, which is an offensive weapon directed towards the Enemy, with praise which is directed towards God. Although it is true that praise is a weapon when it is declaring God's truth, there is a danger of praising to create an effect. We do not praise to win battles; we praise because God is worthy to be praised. The kind of teaching that uses praise as a means to an end has no biblical foundation and is superficial.

In some situations praise releases the presence of God, and his power is demonstrated by bringing a clear victory over the Enemy, as in the case of the Basingstoke minibus. In other situations praise may not bring an outward and obvious effect, but God's power and presence can be just as real. When the early Christians were thrown into the arena, their songs of praise could often be heard above the roar of the crowd. There has been a tendency to think that if you praise God for your troubles and circumstances, they will go away. We praise God *in* our circumstances because he is sovereign over every situation. When we do this the circumstances may not change, but we will.

When we sing our praises to God, we cast up a highway for him in the heavenly places: 'Sing to God, sing praises to His name; cast up a highway for Him who rides through the deserts, whose name is the Lord, and exult before Him' (Ps 68:4). Praise brings us into a spiritual dimension where we affect what happens in heavenly places. We cast up a highway for God to come down and manifest himself.

We must always remember that our focus should be on God. Another tendency is to use praise as a weapon against principalities and powers. Praise which has as its motivation the aim to bind principalities and powers has a wrong focus. There is a danger of unreality in praising to create the effect of binding spiritual beings. There is no biblical precedent for this and there is no way of testing its effectiveness.

Jesus has already bound the strong man. We need to understand the victory of the cross and the power of that victory over Satan. The god of this world is powerful and certainly has a sphere of activity. He is nevertheless defeated. The church has now been invested with authority to make the legal defeat of Satan actual by bringing in the kingdom. As we preach the word, wielding the two-edged sword, proclaiming deliverance and bringing healing, so people will be transferred from the domain of darkness to the kingdom of God. The binding of these spiritual beings, the kings and nobles mentioned in Psalm 149, takes place as we preach the word. Accompanying the word will be the saints giving glory to God with their high praises, rejoicing in all that God is doing in releasing the captives.

Everything we do in the Christian life is an act of warfare against the Enemy. Prayer, evangelism, practical acts of service, counselling and praise and worship. Each time a Christian resists the temptation to lose their temper, feel resentment, or not tell the truth, it is an act of aggression against the Enemy. The problem with the concept of 'praise warfare' is that it limits our motivations for praise and restricts other valid ways in which we overcome the Enemy.

The whole of our life is an aggressive warfare, and every aspect of the Christian life is a weapon against Satan. When we live by the two-edged sword, the word of God, we live by that word in every situation. If we are sick, in financial need, or going through crisis, the promises of God are certain for us. By proclaiming and confessing God's word and declaring who God is in our situations, we are able to stay in victory. Praise and confession of the word are inextricably linked.

Our lives should be lived to the praise of God's glory. He is sovereign over every situation, his Spirit, the Comforter, abides with us. A life of constant communion and praise will put the Enemy to flight, even in the darkest and most trying of circumstances. Whether we are singing a song that is overtly about spiritual warfare, or whether we are singing a soft, gentle love song to Jesus, it is all an expression of the kingdom of God, dispelling the darkness and evil of the domain of Satan. Praise is a weapon, but that is a by-product. Praise does have an effect against the Enemy, but we must watch our motivation. God is to be praised because he is worthy of our praise. The battles belong to God. Let us keep our focus right.

An illustration of the relationship between praise and spiritual warfare can be found in 2 Chronicles chapter 20. Jehoshaphat, the king of Judah, was a good king. He was a man of prayer and he kept the nation in reasonable spiritual health. However, he made the drastic mistake of allying himself to the wicked King Ahab through marriage. Although God had promised the nation freedom from their enemies in the promised land, the promise was conditional on total obedience. Jehoshaphat's folly had made Judah vulnerable, and sure enough the Ammonites began to pose a serious threat.

Fear gripped Jehoshaphat as he realized the vast numbers in the Ammonite army which had allied itself with another hostile nation, the Moabites. Jehoshaphat began to seek God and consulted with the prophets who assured him that the battle was the Lord's and that he would be victorious. The Levites, the musical priests, began to praise the Lord very loudly when they heard this. Jehoshaphat then appointed the musicians and singers to go out before the army. As they went forward singing and praising, God sent ambushments against the enemy who then began fighting among themselves and destroyed each other. Judah was totally victorious without having to fight. No wonder they came back in thanksgiving to the House of the Lord in Jerusalem with their harps, lyres and trumpets.

How did Judah win the battle? Was it through the praising, singing musicians? Is this a valid strategy for spiritual warfare? There was far more to winning this battle than praise and worship. It was rather a matter of people fulfilling their functions obediently: Jehoshaphat prayed and interceded; the prophets declared God's purposes; the people obeyed, and the Levites led the singing with their instruments.

The strategy for overcoming the Enemy and establishing the kingdom is by the people of God living by the whole truth, of which praise and worship is not only an integral but a leading part. As the anointed body is restored and the church begins to function in its priestly, prophetic and kingly roles, so the kingdom will be more firmly established. When the content of praise declares God's word, we can expect certain things to happen in establishing the kingdom. God's power will be released, God's glory will be manifested, and God's presence will be realized. When we grasp this, we should have an expectation that every time God's people gather to offer him praise and worship, the Enemy will be overthrown. When God is enthroned on the praises of his people, Satan's rule is thwarted.

Appendix 1

Songs and Songwriting

I was a young teenager when my first composition was performed. I had entered a contest and written a simple tune arranged for brass instruments. I did not win the competition, but the thrill of hearing my own composition performed by others has never left me. God has imparted the gift of creativity to us, and what better way to see that gift developed than for worship.

Many people ask me how and why I compose worship songs. Do the words come first, or does the tune? How do you write words? Do you need to be a musician to write worship songs? Personally I have found that there is no set formula. The song 'At Your feet we fall' was composed instantaneously. I was reading Revelation chapter 1 and I sat down at the piano, singing the song all the way through. I then hastened to write it down before it was forgotten. 'O Lamb of God' was written as an expression of faith and confidence in God's power to beliver the oppressed, after I had been involved in some ministry to a person who was demonized.

Other songs have suggested themselves as a result of teaching ministry I have brought to my church. Sometimes other people's ministries have prompted a song—the ministry of Terry Virgo has proved a particularly rich source of inspiration. It has been my privilege on many occasions to share the platform with Terry at events like Downs Bible Weeks where he has taught and I have led the worship. I have sought to write songs of a prophetic nature which help to establish what Terry has taught by putting relevant words into people's mouths. An example of such a song is 'Build Your church and heal this land' which accompanied the stirring challenge brought at the 1986 Downs Bible Weeks to see the church built and the nation reached for God.

New songs for old?

With so many new songs available for worship we may well wonder if any more are needed. Is there a place for traditional hymns? Do we need to sing songs more than twice in a meeting?

The major difference between traditional hymns and modern worship songs is in their cultural relevance. Both the musical and poetic structure of hymns speak of an age where the singing of songs and ballads was a popular pastime. The hymns of Isaac Watts and Charles Wesley had a cultural relevance in their day. People were used to their style. The use of popular folk melodies helped to bring the music of the church and the music of the people closer together. The melody for John Bunyan's hymn 'He who would valiant be', commonly known as 'Monks Gate', was originally a popular folk ballad sung in taverns. Frank Houghton's hymn 'Thou who wast rich beyond all splendour, all for loves' sake becamest poor' is set to a tune that was popular on the stage, 'Raise up your glass for wine inspires us and fires us with courage, love and joy'— Hardly a sentiment to be in one's mind during worship!

We are now living in a day when such music and poetic forms have no cultural relevance and so people who have not had a church upbringing (the majority) find it difficult to identify with them. The main problem with traditional hymns is that the music is outdated and that there are too many words for people to take in. This is because we are more accustomed to the structure of modern songs, which is based not on a succession of verses but on simple poetic ideas which are repeated, often with a memorable musical phrase called a 'hook' which helps to plant it firmly in the memory.

However, although traditional hymns may be a cultural anachronism, they still have something to contribute to today's church. Many hymns were born in the fires of revival and express truth that is eternal. If a hymn is to be used in worship, it is preferable if the musicians give it a contemporary interpretation (singing and playing the hymn faster is not necessarily the answer). Care needs to be given to the feel and rhythm. A little imaginative adaptation can breathe life into a dead tune. One example is Keith Green's interpretation of 'Holy, Holy, Holy, Lord God Almighty' to the tune of Nicea (*Songs for the Shepherd*, Word, 1982) For many this hymn to this tune has connotations of turgid school assemblies with reluctance and boredom making a mockery of such wonderful words. By careful phrasing and playing in a contemporary style, Keith Green brings a whole new dimension to a grand hymn that has a timelessness in what it expresses. Notice as well that by changing dated words and phrases the meaning of the song is clearer—very few people today would understand 'which wert and art'! However, not all older tunes will lend themselves to this kind of treatment, so if it doesn't work, it is better not to force it.

The relevance, then, of hymns lies in their capacity to be adapted for contemporary use. If the church is to speak to today's generation, there must be a cultural relevance in the way truth is expressed. Any aspiring songwriter would do well to make a thorough study of hymns, soaking himself in the truths and longings expressed by hymn writers who enjoyed an outpouring of the Spirit yet to be seen in this generation. Could not the same Holy Spirit who inspired Charles Wesley to write, 'Come, Holy Ghost, our heart's inspire; let us Thine influence prove, source of the old prophetic fire, fountain of life and love,' inspire contemporary songwriters with words and melodies which will put the same aspirations in the hearts and on the lips of today's church?

Modern worship songs have proved to be effective because of the immediacy of their appeal, their succinct content, often expressing one or two aspects of truth, and their contemporary relevance. They are just as much a phenomenon of the creative Spirit of God as the traditional hymns, and although the words may lack the poetic qualities of hymns, that is not necessarily a drawback as most of them are based on Scripture. Thus, when a worship song is repeated several times in a meeting, the truth that is expressed becomes absorbed by the people singing. Repetition is only wrong when it is meaningless. Whereas a hymn might cover several points of doctrine, a worship song might only cover one. If another truth is to be expressed, then another song is started up.

Contemporary worship songs may not have such a long life as hymns. Only a few will stand the test of time and so there needs to be a fresh flow of new songs. The truths remain constant while the music expressing those truths changes. It is possible, of course, to write hymns in the language and music of today; Graham Kendrick, in particular, has done this to great effect.

The role of the songwriter

The songwriter can be a prophetic voice to the church, putting into song what God is saying. Over the last twenty years there have been seasons of songs focusing on a particular aspect of truth. There was a period when many songs were written about Christian fellowship and our life in God together. Songs about the kingdom of God, building the church, and reaching the world for God, have come in waves. What people sing helps to establish and clarify their vision.

People absorb truth as they sing, thus singing can be a form of meditation. As Scripture is vocalized, people grow strong in their faith. Proclaiming truths about God's Fatherhood, our sonship, and eternal security can help establish these doctrines in the heart. Naturally, they are no substitute for

Bible study and meditation, but they can greatly enhance what is being gleaned from the word, helping the truth of the Bible to be translated into worship in the heart.

The songwriter can also reflect and interpret what God is doing. When a new song is taught to a congregation, it can bring freshness into the worship time and keep truths alive in people's minds. There may be a particular teaching series that inspires the songwriter to complement the teaching ministry. The songwriter has a prophetic and a teaching ministry in that he envisions with God's purpose and helps to establish truth in people's lives.

The craft of the songwriter

I find that most songs are written as I spend time in worship and waiting on God. I may have been meditating on a passage of Scripture, or spending time in prayer. Writing songs is a subjective matter to which each songwriter brings his own distinctiveness and creativity. Below are some guidelines which will help to shape an original idea, though they should not be treated as rules.

The words

(1) Avoid clichés.
(2) Avoid sentimentality.
(3) Avoid obscure poetic imagery.
(4) Make sure the words have a rhythmic scan.
(5) Don't have too many words.
(6) Check your theology.
(7) Check your grammar.

I have found it helpful to write down the essence of the song in one sentence. If it is not possible to give a pithy description of the song, it probably has too much content. The words of Scripture are an excellent source, but give attention to the context. Putting Scripture into lines of poetry, or at least lines that scan rhythmically, is a useful method of writing words.

The music

(1) *The hook*

The melodic hook is the part of the tune that people remember, and so a good musical catch-phrase with appropriate words will help establish the tune. It will also give you a reference point as you are composing.

E.g. In the song 'Emmanuel' (*Songs of Fellowship* vol.3, no. 352, Kingsway 1985) the hook phrase is 'God is with us, God is with us'.

EXAMPLE 1

(2) *Sequences*

Sequences are a way in which an original melodic idea can be developed, bringing a unity and stability to the song. An excellent example of the use of sequences can be found in Graham Kendrick's song 'Meekness and Majesty' (*Make Way*, Kingsway 1986).

EXAMPLE 2

Notice a slight departure from the sequence creating melodic variation and interest.

(3) *Form*

A song should have a definite structure and form—this prevents too many musical ideas from cluttering the song. Phrases should normally be in groupings of four or eight bars.

The most common structure for a song is 'A B A' (the letters representing a melody of 16-24 bars). An example of A B A is 'O Lord, you are my light' (*Songs of Fellowship* vol.2, no. 273, Kingsway 1983):

A   Lord, You are my light
B   For my life is hidden
A   Lord, You are my light

It is probably most effective to restrict the form to not more than three main ideas. A B A, A B A C A, A B C B A and A B A C A are all effective structures for songs.

(4) *Answering phrases*

Place one musical phrase in juxtaposition with another as an answering phrase. This can be done successfully between men and women.

(5) *Two-part songs*

Two-part songs can lift congregational singing in a very satisfying way, bringing a whole new dimension into corporate worship. The biggest danger in writing two-part songs is that they can sound contrived. The parts should not be composed separately without reference to each other as there will be the risk of melodic clashes. Try to develop the skill of hearing both parts simultaneously in the head. Make sure when the song divides that the starting note for both parts is easy to pitch.

(6) *The range*

The most effective range for congregational singing is from C to E.

EXAMPLE 3

Notes below C will not be heard and notes above E will cause
people to strain. Keep the melody as much in the middle of
the range as possible. Awkward leaps should also be avoided.

(7) *Originality*

All good songs have a touch of originality about them, an
unusual chord, or an interesting melodic phrase. It is
important that anything like this is an integral part of the
song, and not added in a contrived fashion. There are many
ways in which a song can be given a touch of the unusual. A
change of rhythm, or a particular harmonic flavour, can be
added after the song has been written. The use of major and
minor seventh chords can add colour.

Releasing the song

Once the song has been written, it is best to get a group of
people together to try it out before introducing it to a congregation. This will iron out any difficulties, and adjustments can
then be made. Don't be afraid to make changes, and listen to
other people's assessments of what you write.

Don't be discouraged if a song does not appeal; keep
writing. Over the years my wastepaper-bin has been filled
with songs that originally seemed good, but then went off the
boil. The gift of songwriting can make a significant contribution to the worshipping church. I have found that people
enjoy learning new songs, and as God continues to restore the
church, I am sure that many new songs will express truths that
God is bringing to his people.

Appendix 2

Worship Words

Tozer called worship 'the missing jewel'. The different words used in scripture for worship explore that jewel from many angles, revealing a colour, sparkle and rich variety that should be reflected in both personal and corporate times of worship. True worship springs from deep within the heart, resulting in a life of obedience, joyful acclamations, and times of hushed awe as we approach the King with the intimacy of a kiss.

Halal

To be boastful, to praise, to celebrate. *Halal* is the source of the word 'hallelujah', meaning 'Praise the Lord'. *Yah* is an abbreviated form of *Yahweh*, the Old Testament name for God. Psalms 113-118 are referred to as the Hallel Psalms. They give praise to God for Israel's deliverance from Egypt, and they were traditionally sung on the eve of the Passover celebrations.

Hallelujah can be used as an explosion of enthusiasm, rather like sports fans when a goal is scored. *Halal* is found

138

more than 160 times in the Old Testament.

Yadah

To give thanks, to praise. The root of this word suggests the extended hand. *Yadah* therefore implies worshipping with raised hands.

The word originated in the story of the birth of Jacob's son, Judah (Gen 29:35-36): 'And she conceived again and bore a son and said, "This time I will praise the Lord." Therefore she named him Judah.'

Yadah also means to acknowledge in public or to praise the Lord publicly: 'I will give Thee thanks in the great congregation; I will praise Thee among a mighty throng' (Ps 35:18).

Todah

To give thanks. This word is often used to indicate songs of thanksgiving: 'That I may proclaim with the voice of thanksgiving, and declare all Thy wonders' (Ps 26:7). 'With the voice of joy and thanksgiving, a multitude keeping festival' (Ps 42:4).

When Nehemiah had completed the building of the walls of Jerusalem, he appointed two choirs to march and process around the walls. They are described as thanksgiving choirs (Neh 12:31, 38).

Tehillah

A song of praise particularly extolling deeds which are worthy of praise (*Tehillim* is the Hebrew title for the book of Psalms.) It also refers to a person's attributes: 'He is your praise and He is your God, who has done these great and awesome things for you which your eyes have seen' (Deut 10:21).

Tehillah means praising God for who he is and for his actions. It also means to publicly praise and laud by singing: 'O Thou who art enthroned upon the praises of Israel. . . . I will tell of Thy name to my brethren; in the midst of the assembly I will praise Thee' (Ps 22:3, 22; cf. Heb 2:12).

Tehillah is also a technical musical term for a song of praise, as in Psalm 145.

Barak

To bless. This word is generally used to speak of God's covenant in pouring out his blessing on mankind, but it is also used as an expression of praise: 'Blessed be God Most High . . . who has delivered your enemies into your hand' (Gen 14:20). We are able to bless God by not forgetting the ways in which he has blessed us: 'Bless the Lord, O my soul; and all that is within me, bless His holy name. Bless the Lord, O my soul, and forget none of His benefits' (Ps 103:1-2).

Zamar

Literally, to touch the strings (of a harp or lyre). It refers to praising the Lord in song, with harmony and musical accompaniment: 'My heart is steadfast, O God; I will sing, I will sing praises, even with my soul. Awake, harp and lyre; I will awaken the dawn' (Ps 108:1).

Shabach

To congratulate, to speak well of. It suggests triumphantly celebrating, glorying and shouting: 'Praise the Lord, all nations; laud Him, all peoples' (Ps 117:1)

Samach

To be glad, to rejoice. This word implies an outburst of spontaneous joy which overflows into some physical action. Emotion is expressed in singing, dancing and the playing of musical instruments. 'Be glad in the Lord and rejoice you righteous ones, and shout for joy all you who are upright in heart' (Ps 32:11). The word is also used for the way God rejoices: 'Let the glory of the Lord endure forever; let the Lord be glad in His works' (Ps 104:31).

Siys

To be bright, to leap with mirth. 'Let all who seek Thee rejoice and be glad in Thee' (Ps 40:16).

Giyl

To rejoice, to cry out and be glad: 'Yet I will exult in the Lord, I will rejoice in the God of my salvation' (Hab 3:18).

Shacah

To bow down in reverence, to prostrate oneself: 'So the people believed; and when they heard that the Lord was concerned about the sons of Israel and that He had seen their affliction, then they bowed low and worshipped' (Ex 4:31). It is the word commonly used to denote coming before God in worship.

Ruah

To raise a shout, a battle cry, a jubilant shout of joy: 'O come, let us sing for joy to the Lord; let us shout joyfully to the rock of our salvation' (Ps 95:1).

Quara

To call, or proclaim. 'I have proclaimed glad tidings of righteousness in the great congregation' (Ps 40:9).

These Hebrew words reveal different aspects of praise and worship, and give some insight into Old Testament worship.

There are also a number of Greek words covering worship in the New Testament.

Proskuneo

This is a very common New Testament word for worship; it means to come towards to kiss. Originally the word had to do with kissing the earth as part of pagan worship, but gradually the idea changed to an inner attitude rather than an outward gesture. It is an expression of intimacy and adoration (Mt 2:2; Lk 4:8; Jn 4:20-24; Rev 4:10; 19:10; 22:9.)

Sebomai

Originally this word was used to express the idea of shrinking away from the gods because of reverence and fear. It is a word which emphasizes feelings of reverence and awe in the presence of God (Mt 15:9; Mk 7:7; Acts 16:14; 18:7).

Latreuo

This word is used in Philippians 3:3 for worship: 'For we are the true circumcision, who worship in the Spirit of God and glory in Christ Jesus and put no confidence in the flesh.' The use of *latreuo* emphasizes that worship is not only an inner attitude, but also an outward manifestation of this attitude in righteous living. *Latreuo* implies worship demonstrated by lifestyle.

This word is used three times in connection with the sacrificial ministry of the priests in Hebrews 9: 'Now when these things have been thus prepared, the priests are continually entering the outer tabernacle, performing the divine worship' (Heb 9:6). In Romans 12:1 the word is used again to signify the life of a Christian as a living sacrifice. Our 'spiritual service of worship' is the worship we render to God demonstrated by our lifestyle. We continually present ourselves to God in a condition of inner sacrifice resulting in obedient Christian behaviour.

Chaira

To rejoice. Originally this word implied the joy of celebrating at a festival. It is a joy that is expressed and sustained, even through persecution and trial, because of the hope that is before the Christian (Mt 5:12; Lk 1:14; Phil 1:4; 2:28-29; 3:1; 4:10).

Agaillo

To rejoice greatly, to exult, to lift up. It refers to a joy that is demonstrated (Mt 5:12; Lk 1:47; Jn 5:35; 1 Pet 1:8; Acts 16:34).

Appendix 3

Methods of Orchestration

In all but the highest level of musicianship, the secret of effective orchestration is to work with the limitations and strengths of the musicians you have. Consequently, I can really only give general guidelines which you must apply to your own specific situation.

Extemporary

This is the most common form of playing in worship where, with a foundation of keyboard or guitar, the other musicians 'improvise', or make up their own parts, by working around the melody line and accompanying chords. Although not strictly a form of orchestration as such, its effectiveness still depends on a strong element of overall control and direction. When extemporizing together, all the instrumentalists should keep their parts simple or the sound will be too busy, the overall effect will be blurred, and the phrasing and dynamics of the song will be lost—by far the most common fault with this form of playing.

Having said that, one should still seek to encourage musicians to use their instruments to their full extent by sometimes having one melodic improvisation featuring the gifting and style of a particular player. In one song it may be appropriate to have a driving guitar sound, in another a haunting melodic oboe or violin improvisation may be more effective. Different songs lend themselves to powerful interpretation by a particular instrument/instrumentalist. The same is true within individual songs where several different tones and colours can be achieved by selective improvisation.

Mutual understanding and sensitivity are essential among your musicians when improvising together, and can only really be gained through regular practice together. Inevitably, players come from different musical backgrounds and have different styles of playing. You may find yourself with a rock guitarist, a 'trad' jazz trumpet player, a classically trained oboist, and a 'pub-style' pianist, and it will take time—together with an attitude of mutual submission, respect and care—to nurture an effective ministering group of musicians who work well together.

Simple written orchestrations

In practical terms, you may find the effect achieved by extemporaneous playing severely limited, particularly with a larger group of musicians. You may also have a number of competent players who cannot improvise and really need something to 'read'. In either case, simple arrangements of songs can produce very pleasing and powerful effects.

The three ingredients of music—rhythm, melody and harmony—need to be given special attention in simple orchestration. The instruments which provide a rhythmic and harmonic foundation are guitar and keyboard. A keyboard is the preferable foundation because of its versatility and carrying power. The guitar can give a foundation if the player has a wide chord vocabulary, a good rhythmic sense, and the sound of the guitar is able to carry. Ideally a contemporary worship band should have as its foundation bass, drums, and keyboard, which together will establish the essential rhythm and chordal basis of the song. Having established the harmonic and rhythmic foundation, other melodic instruments can be added. Providing the group of musicians can provide rhythm, melody and harmony, it is possible to orchestrate.

All you need is a twelve-stave A4 spiral-back manuscript book, a pencil, and a rubber. It is best to write in pencil first, which is much easier to correct than ink. A4 twelve manuscript is best because of its legibility. Always write neatly and carefully, making sure that notes in a space do not encroach on the line above or the line below.

Simple orchestration is designed to give two alternative parts to the melody. These two parts can be played on any melody instrument. Three lines of manuscript paper are needed. The bottom line is for the melody, with the chords.

EXAMPLE 1

Insert the melody, making the bar lines extend the whole width of the stave. Put in the key signature and time signature.

EXAMPLE 2

Jesus You are the Radiance

A basic knowledge of chords is vital for this exercise. Each note in the melody is harmonized with a chord. Each chord has two other basic notes, and some chords have others added, e.g. a 7th or a sus4. It may be helpful to write out each chord on a separate piece of manuscript paper as a reference point (Example 3). Where a chord has a different bass note, the convention is to draw a line between the chord and the bass note, e.g. C/F means a C chord with F bass; Bb/F means a Bb chord with F bass.

EXAMPLE 3

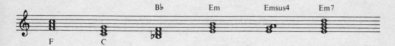

Take notes in the chord, differing from the notes in the melody, and write an alternative line to the melody.

EXAMPLE 4

Try to keep each part as melodically interesting as possible. Avoid too many intervals and keep the smoothest line the music will allow. An alternative method is to take a book like *Songs of Fellowship* and use the inner parts in the piano arrangement for melodic instruments.

The best way to learn orchestration is to write out the parts, then play the composition. If it sounds right, it is right; if it sounds wrong, then try to diagnose the fault and correct it.

When we first formed a worship band at Clarendon seven years ago, each instrumentalist had a loose-leaf folder with the melody line, chord charts, the words of the song and two alternative lines to play as shown in the examples. This meant that all the instruments had something to play and they blended together well.

Advanced orchestration

1. In classical style

This uses melodic instruments harmonically and needs a good number of instrumentalists. Combinations of instruments provide the tone colour and, if there are enough instrumentalists with a wide range from the bass end to the upper, then the combination can be entirely self-sufficient (Example 5).

Note: When copying parts from the full score, make sure that the transposing instruments are in the right key (clarinets in Bb up a tone; trumpets in Bb up a tone; horns in F up a fifth; tenor sax in Bb up a tone; alto sax in Eb up a sixth).

With practice it should be possible to write the parts already transposed onto the full score.

2. Contemporary orchestration/arranging

Again, the basic building-block for contemporary arranging is the rhythm section. Bass guitar, drums and keyboard and/or guitarist provide the foundation. Instruments added to this lend colour and interest, but do not play all the time. Rhythmic figures called riffs, usually played by brass or guitar, can add interest.

In a church setting, musicians should go for as wide a range of styles as possible. Each instrument should be exploited to its full potential. A careful working out of parts with consideration to balance, colour and style will enhance accompaniment to worship.

EXAMPLE 5

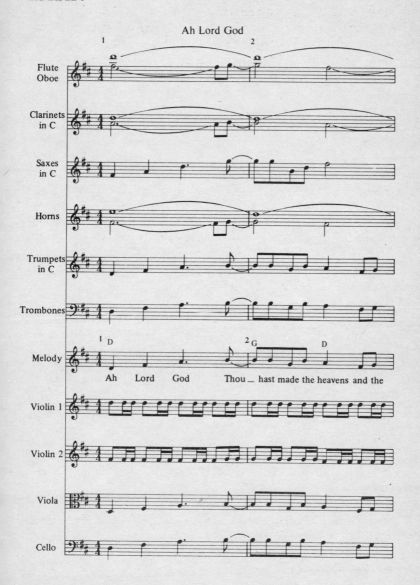

Ah Lord God

earth by Thy Great pow-er._____ Ah Lord God Thou_

_hast made the heavens and the earth by thine out-stretched arm.

Some ideas for instrumentalists

Strings

  (1) Long notes held over several bars (in the style of a string synth, a style of string playing common to middle-of-the-road pop music).
  (2) remeloes.
  (3) Rhythmic strumming effect, played against others playing the melody.
  (4) Pizzicato.
  (5) Melodic counter melodies.

Flute

  (1) Descants.
  (2) Melody.
  (3) Trills on long notes at cadence points.
  (4) Jazz improvisation.
  (5) Doubling the bass line (if used sparingly, this can be effective).

Oboe

This instrument has a very plaintive sound and can penetrate well. The oboe is also an effective solo instrument.

  (1) Melody.
  (2) Descant.
  (3) Improvised arpeggio lines.

Clarinet

This instrument can be used in the same way as the flute and oboe. It is often effective in the lower register in worshipful songs, and in quick runs and arpeggios.

Trumpets, saxes, trombone and horn can all be used for fanfares, jazz riffs and melodic playing.

Trumpet

  (1) Fanfares.

Trombone

(1) Counter melody.
(2) Riffs.
(3) Muted (very effective with the oboe).

Horn

(1) Long notes sustained through several bars.
(2) Melody.
(3) Counter melody.

Saxes

These can be very expressive.
(1) Riffs
(2) Jazz improvisation.
(3) Melody and counter melody.

Bass guitar/Bass

(1) Provide a harmonic foundation.
(2) Create rhythmic interest. Watch the volume, and don't be too busy. The bass guitar should not be played like a lead guitar—don't play the tune.
(3) Double bass is better pizzicato than bowed as this helps the rhythm.
(4) Pay careful attention to the inversions of chords. If the chord chart says C/E, make sure that the bass is playing the underneath note. A wrong inversion can alter the character of the chord.

Guitars

(1) Provide rhythmic drive.
(2) Finger-picking arpeggio style (for gentler songs).
(3) Electric lead.

Synthesizers

Contemporary music has moved away from the electric organ sound and synthesizers have become an integral part of the music scene. They can substitute for missing instruments and provide a wide range of tone colours and effects.

Keyboards

Congregations find it easiest to sing against a clear keyboard sound. There is no real substitute for an acoustic piano or a good quality electric piano.

Percussion

The percussion section of a worship band is important because it helps to give a solid rhythm and can add interest and colour.

The kit player needs skill and discipline to play in praise and worship. Rhythmic drive and volume are not synonymous. It takes hours of practice for a drummer to play skilfully at a sensible volume. The rhythm section should rehearse together, concentrating on keeping a steady tempo and beginning and ending songs. Many amateur drummers are too busy with too many frills. Simplicity is most effective in worship.

There is a whole range of other percussion instruments that can add colour. The biblical 'loud cymbals' can evoke a sense of the majesty of God. The tambourine is a musical instrument, and the indiscriminate banging that happens in some congregations should be corrected by somebody who knows how to play one, giving a lead from the musicians. Other percussion instruments are cabasa, bells, guira, claves, triangle and various hand drums.

The percussionist should rehearse with the kit player to work out rhythmic phrasing. A good percussion section working together producing a tight, well-rehearsed foundation will help to release people into dance in the congregation.

Postscript

If the Holy Spirit should come again upon us as in earlier times, visiting church congregations with the sweet but fiery breath of Pentecost, we would be greater Christians and holier souls. Beyond that we would also be greater poets, greater artists, and greater lovers of God and of His universe.[15]

We are living in exciting days, with the wind of God blowing across the nations of the earth. God's purpose is for an end-time church that is glorious and powerful, a testimony to the power of the cross, the resurrection and Pentecost.

Worship is an integral part of God's purpose for his church. Simply singing new songs or going through the motions of the mechanics of worship will not produce the life that God desires. God longs for living churches that are unfettered by the chains of stale tradition. A biblical vision and structure will produce a people who are attaining the fullness of the stature of Christ. Such churches will provide opportunities for all to come to their full potential in their gifting, and this will include anointed creativity. Such churches will also provide a radical alternative to this sin-sick world, and will help to prepare for the coming of the King.

Notes

Chapter 1

1. Donald Jay Grout, *A History of Western Music* (London, Dent, 1960) p.9.
2. *Ibid.*, p.14.
3. Alec Harman, *Man and His Music Part 1* (London, Barrie and Rockliffe, 1962) p.13.
4. E.M. Blaiklock, transl., *The Confessions of St. Augustine* (London, Hodder and Stoughton, 1983) p.272.

Chapter 2

5. F.F. Bruce, *The Spreading Flame* (Exeter, Paternoster, 1958) p.79.
6. Justin Martyr, *First Apologie* (c.152).
7. M.A. Smith, *From Christ to Constantine* (Leicester, Inter-varsity Press, 1971) pp.148-9.
8. Donald Jay Grout, *A History of Western Music* (London, Dent, 1960) p.26.
9. E.H. Broadbent, *The Pilgrim Church* (Basingstoke, Pickering and Inglis, 1974) p.292.

10. Eifion Evans, *The Welsh Revival of 1904* (Bridgend, Evangelical Press of Wales, 1974) p.111.
11. *Ibid.*, p.127.

Chapter 3

12. Louis Berkhof, *Systematic Theology* (Edinburgh, Banner of Truth, 1971) p.357.

Chapter 4

13. Ralph Martin, *Worship in the Early Church* (Basingstoke, Marshall, Morgan and Scott, 1964) p.45.

Chapter 6

14. Joseph Gelineau, *Voices and Instruments in Christian Worship* (Tunbridge Wells, Burns and Oates, 1964) p.37.

Postscript

15. A.W. Tozer, *Whatever Happened to Worship* (Eastbourne, Kingsway, 1986) p.37.

Worship

by Graham Kendrick

*Hymns—choruses; silence—noise;
kneeling—dancing; liturgy—freedom.*

Whatever our personal preferences in worship, this
book sets out to discover what *God* is looking for, as our
worship is primarily for him. What part should worship
play in our lives? And how does this affect the way we
relate together as God's people?

Whether you are a leader of worship or see yourself as
playing a more passive role, this book is designed to
help you experience greater depth and meaning in your
highest calling—to worship the living God.

Graham Kendrick has had many years' experience of leading worship
in both small and large Christian gatherings. He is widely
acknowledged as one of Britain's leading singer-songwriters, being
well known for his many songs of praise and worship.

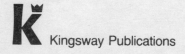 Kingsway Publications

Real Worship

by Warren Wiersbe

If you long for a greater sense of wonder in worship;

— if you want to be more effective in witness and warfare;

— if you are concerned more with realities than labels;

— if you love to call God *God* — and nothing less —

this book will encourage you in the direction you are going.

Warren Wiersbe is General Director of the Back to the Bible Broadcast in the USA. His books and teaching at conferences have earned him the reputation of being a "pastor's pastor," and in *Real Worship* he demonstrates his ability to get right to the heart of an issue and let the word of God make its own challenge to our traditions, our churches, and our lives.

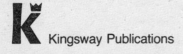 Kingsway Publications